BIGNESS

How Successful Leaders
Grow into New Roles

SANDER A. FLAUM

LEADERSHAPE PUBLISHING

2009

Published by LeaderShape Publishing
630 Park Avenue, Suite 9B
New York, NY 10065
© 2009 by Sander A. Flaum

Printed in the United States of America

First Printing

ISBN 978-1-44951-177-7

TABLE OF CONTENTS

Foreword

For those who read the book Dad and I did together five years ago, *The 100-Mile Walk*, you know that while I respected the leadership practices that he espoused, I differed with his approach. Five years later, I read an even more reflective work: one that simultaneously holds the promise and pitfalls of leadership in the same hand and expresses each clearly, without sentimentality. *Big Shoes: How Successful Leaders Grow Into New Roles* is a pithy compendium of a leader's life distilled down to what's necessary. It's a great little how-to book, but it's more because it is nuanced with questions of "why."

To be a leader, you have to give up a lot: time, freedom, reflection, and solitude, to name but a few. It is a job that requires constant action. And, often, you will be criticized for those actions.

So why would you want to take it on? My father makes a good case for purpose, legacy, love of a cause, and wanting to leave the world a better place as compelling reasons to lead. But he doesn't sugarcoat the drawbacks and the difficulties of balancing the pressures of leading a major company with simply living life—like doing the dishes at home and helping your child with her homework. Choosing work over time with a friend strains your relationship, yet being relentless in the first 100 days of your leadership position can build a great precedent for future success. Both are true.

Business leadership makes unreasonable demands of everyone—the leader, subordinates, the leader's family. And a great leader can bring unanticipated—and remarkable—results to the company with an effort of single-minded passion.

Are the trade offs worth it? That's for you to decide. *Big Shoes* doesn't pick sides; however, it does lay down the truth. If you want to lead, or have been at it for a while and feel the need to re-energize and gain an extended view, take just three hours and read this. I did. It helped me confirm that leadership is neither good nor bad. It simply is what it is: a commitment of tremendous proportion and effort. And taking it on requires a particular kind of sensibility, a sensibility that Dad has always had. He articulates it in *Big Shoes* with the precision and wisdom of a man who has honed his craft after years of practice.

—Jonathon Flaum
August 2009

Introduction

Lace Up

STOCKS FLUCTUATE WILDLY. Currencies are unpredictable. Energy prices are bipolar.

The broad economic and administrative challenges facing today's leaders are virtually unprecedented. Few mistakes will go unnoticed, and even fewer will be forgiven.

A confluence of events has focused today's watchdogs on business leaders. People at the top of American business and nonprofits are under microscopic surveillance. Globalization, broad economic strife and an increasingly populist sensibility have created a highly volatile environment.

First came the scandals of the early 2000s: Enron and WorldCom. They drew outrage from the public as thousands of people lost thousands of dollars, as pensions disappeared, and as America's faith in the "fair and square" nature of good business leaders evaporated.

The Sarbanes-Oxley Act that followed those scandals offered some promise; it helped lay the groundwork for executive accountability, restoring some faith in corporate accounting and in the government's ability to keep tabs on the titans of industry.

Yet almost no time elapsed before the corporate greed and poor decision making underlying the subprime mortgage debacle triggered a credit paralysis and a full blown economic downturn: less than ten years later, it all came crashing down. For many, that was the last straw. Scandal, greedy CEOs and their Boards of Directors and the rapid decline into a recession left Americans confused, angry, and highly skeptical of all corporate, government, and even nonprofit institutions and those in charge of running them.

Today, chief executives and their direct reports face unprecedented scrutiny and often sacrifice pride, sleep, and bonuses only to be made into scapegoats and examples of unethical behavior.

Moreover, business people are not the only ones feeling the heat. In Washington, newly elected officials and regulators and the system they belong to have never been so squarely under the gun. The recent changes in the executive leadership of the United States and global business are indicative of stakeholders' dwindling patience for mistakes.

No industry's leaders can hide from the people's microscope. In filmmaking, directors are routinely replaced. In academia, university presidents are often taken to task for public gaffes. In the National Football League, each season ends with talk of the "coaching carousel," wherein coaches who have failed to deliver with one team are shown the door and hope to catch on with another.

Welcome to leadership in the new era. Colleagues, employees, stakeholders, subordinates, constituents, and fans may not always know what they want, but they often come to realize—with startling speed—that their current leader just won't cut it.

WHY READ THIS BOOK NOW?

Here is the good news: for all of the negative attention given to subpar executives and government heads, talented, high-integrity leaders still need to step in and up. Just as a sluggish economy has made America less patient about corporate fouls, it has also made the nation and the world hungry for A+ leaders, those who will help guide their organizations out of the darkness and into a new era of profitability and success.

This book is for people who want to be that kind of leader. It is for the rising star, leading his first company of fifteen people out of a low-rent space and accompanied by a checkbook with $10,000 of seed money. It is for the seasoned veteran who finds herself at the top of a firm with high expectations and little tolerance for failure. It is for the ambitious entrepreneur struggling for funds to grow earth-friendly produce and the chief executive of a nonprofit working hard to feed the poor. It is for anyone hungry for the proven leadership skills that drive an organization to the top. It's for you!

We'll begin with some critical and sometimes renegade ideas about personal work and time management to instantly influence your day-to-day activities. Then we'll look at techniques for keeping your staff motivated and inspired. We'll cover strategies for getting ahead individually and staying ahead of the curve. We'll conclude with a discussion on sowing the seeds for the future of your organization and tips for maintaining a work–life balance.

Together we'll look at some of the most valuable lessons I've learned on the job as the chief executive of a successful global advertising and strategic consulting firm, drawing on more than forty years in the pharmaceutical industry and in academia, where I've made a lifelong study of the world's most effective and ineffective leaders. Some of what you'll be reading grew out of columns and articles I've written and my responses to readers, as well as my work at the Fordham University Graduate School of Business as founder and chairman of the Fordham Leadership Forum.

Probably like you, I like my intakes fast and don't believe in wasting time. This book should take you about three hours to read and process. However, it's the implied homework—the practice, practice, practice—that may take time. As my colleague and favorite strategist likes to say, "Don't punish me for being quick to the solution (and don't pay me by the hour)."

As you speed-read your way through each chapter, I urge you to take a moment after each section to think about the ways in which the best practices I relate might be relevant to your own life, your own firm. What's the crystallizing thought for you in each section, and how can you apply it to your workplace quickly?

Above all, I hope you enjoy this book. During challenging times, it's easy to forget that leaders should embrace new strategies and perspectives and remain focused on the horizon. I hope these pages serve to restore some of your optimism and get you eager to try out new ideas.

Happy reading.

CHAPTER 1
You're Hired. Now What?

S TARTING A NEW JOB in today's economic climate is a lot like stepping into the front lines of a war zone. Every day you'll be under attack by new combatants, face new challenges, and come to grips with unforeseen losses. And every day your survival will hinge on your instincts, your preparedness and your ability to build an A+ team. If you're reading this book, there's a good chance you've got your combat boots on. It's time to break them in and begin the tour.

For many first-time presidents, unit heads and division directors, entrepreneurs and social venturers, the idea of running a business operation is daunting, to say the least. This is especially true today, when so many promotions are born out of dismissals. It's natural for that early rush of excitement to dovetail into a stomach full of butterflies. Many of you may have had at least some management experience, but no matter how autonomous your former branch or division was, there is simply no substitute for having the buck for the entire organization stop at your desk.

What's important is to be as prepared for your new role as you can be. That means having a firm grasp of your new division or organization, navigating a tumultuous adjustment phase (the honeymoon period is a myth), and possessing stellar work habits to carry you through your day confidently and efficiently. It also means instilling your people with those same winning practices.

You might be thinking: "Sander, please. I've just been hired to run a five-thousand-person multinational. Before this, I ran the Bangkok office for three years, during which time I boosted margins by 20 percent. Believe me, I've got the skills to pay the bills."

And you might be right, in which case, go ahead and skim this chapter. However, I urge you to consider that just because your old ways got you into this job does not mean they will keep you from losing it.

In this section, we'll take a look at what you should be doing during your first few months on the job—a stressful, volatile time for any new leader, especially during these stressful, volatile times—and we'll make sure you've got solid, proven working habits for the calmer days that follow.

Let's get started.

Spring Into the 100-Day Dash

When President Obama took the oath of office, he wasted little time before signing new executive orders, setting new policies into motion, and assuring Americans that he would make good on his campaign promise of change.

Here's what he did on Day One: established new restrictions on the lobbying in Washington, reversed a Bush-era policy that gave agencies more power to veil their documents, and froze salaries in the Executive Branch to demonstrate national solidarity.

Obama did not stop there. A week of his administration had not yet elapsed before he ordered the shutdown of the American prison at Guantanamo Bay, outlined new proposed regulations for the financial industry, held six meetings with his economic advisors, and repealed a restriction on funding to organizations that offer or promote abortions abroad.

For better or for worse, change had come to Washington. And here it was, streaming out of the White House, one headline after the next.

Over the years, I have endorsed a similar approach when taking over a new leadership position. In the first 100 days, I have argued, new bosses should hit the ground running by showing up with a plan, getting a first-rate staff in place, notching some early wins, and communicating a vision to investors and employees. It's a schedule that instills confidence in your subordinates, fear in your competitors, and momentum in your share price. Get to work early, and everybody wins.

Get to work late (or even on time), and you risk a big loss. Today's boards and stakeholders have far less patience for dumb mistakes, and your new title probably didn't come with training wheels. In a less-than-stellar economy, errors are magnified because opportunity costs are greater. Every decision you make means more today than it might have fifteen years ago. The stakes are higher, the competition is greater and the consequences of failure are more immediately obvious.

With so much riding on even your earliest initiative, you would be wise to take this advice: don't wait until the job actually begins before going to work.

In the corporate world, studies of Fortune 500 companies show that 40 percent of those who take on leadership positions will fail in their first eighteen months. Nonprofits may take a little longer, but not much. My belief is you win or lose in the first 100 days—a little more than a fiscal quarter. That means you should leave behind the day-to-day routines and go all out to maximize results during your first few months on the job. Do yourself and your new organization a favor and get a running start; begin as soon as possible, preferably on the day you receive the offer (Obama and his transition team in many ways took office in November).

Not everyone agrees. In fact, one *Financial Times* columnist used Obama's first half-week on the job to question the value of bringing that same zero-to-sixty attitude to the business world. On Inauguration Day, he wrote that, for CEOs, "100-day plans are usually a mistake," and that, barring emergencies, newbies would be wise to take some time adjusting to their new offices before rolling out new initiatives.

The columnist argues that new managers "just do not know enough" to make informed decisions that could shake up their companies during their first three months on the job. Without having spoken to customers and employees, he says, new leaders will not be able to fully comprehend the needs of their company, nor will they be able to get a leadership team in place that meets those needs.

However, any leader worth his salt will have spoken to customers and employees long before he shows up to work. Most firms will ensure this during their hiring process. A good board of directors or search committee will drill potential candidates on their ability to assess the company's deficiencies and to express a plan to address them. If the candidate cannot demonstrate a working knowledge of the unique demands of the business, if she is unfamiliar with its customer base and staff, then her résumé should have been discarded before the second interview. In other words, board vetting should guarantee that an organization's new leader knows enough about her new position's challenges to select a management team that advances the mission.

The columnist also says that new leaders should not feel compelled to offer a plan of action on their first day on the job. Instead, he says, they can promise to "spend the early months going around listening and learning."

Can you blame shareholders, employees, and citizens if they are skeptical of the leader who pledges to listen and learn early without offering much in the way of substance?

Let's look back at the White House. On February 22, 2001, a month into his presidency, George W. Bush promised to "listen to the commanders in the field" in Iraq after an air strike that intended to secure air space. The next day,

Bush assured the press corps "prior to the formulation of any [Middle East] policy, we will have listened" to "our friends and folks in the Middle East."

Two months later, at the Summit of the Americas meeting in Quebec City, designed to foster cooperation between the U.S. and its neighbors, the President said, "I am most thankful for the generous hospitality each leader showed me. I listened a lot; I learned a lot."

Then, on May 11, talking about gas prices: "If anybody thinks they've got a good idea, I'll listen."

Then, in October, a month after the terrorist attacks in New York and Washington: "I think I listened to probably three or four hours of discussions about our campaign against terrorism. And there was a very strong support for our activities."

Now, if a business or community leader were to say this during the recession, he would inspire about as much confidence as he would declaring a particular initiative a "slam dunk" or celebrating another with "mission accomplished."

Americans and international stakeholders are simply more demanding of their leaders today. They need to hear what the big the idea is, and they need to see it executed without delay.

When Alan Mulally was named the President and CEO of Ford in September 2006, he broke out his expansive restructuring plan—an update to Ford's "Way Forward"—within the first two months of his arrival. By the second quarter of 2007, the firm had turned profitable and remains the most financially stable automaker in Detroit. Granted, Ford shares took a hit with the market downturn, but they clearly outperformed General Motors.

Newly appointed business heads, novice or experienced managers, and new or seasoned executives would be wise to follow President Obama's example. Prepare for the new post so extensively you can walk into your new office and immediately get things done. Otherwise, you're liable to be ousted, and it won't take your constituents four years.

Getting on the Mark for Day One

Start with due diligence. Look especially for what's worth saving. Business may have been flat; shareholders may have been disappointed; top performers may be circulating résumés "just in case." The same forces that created the management change that propelled you into a corner office may have been quietly wreaking havoc on the company. There's no time for a "wait-and-see" approach before probing for answers.

Richard Notebaert, who led Qwest at a time when the company was plagued with dismal financials, a sinking stock price, and an SEC inquiry, says it's important to prioritize from the get-go. "You have to triage," he says. "First, fix the balance sheet and get the revenue going. Then, sort out the legal and regulatory issues."

In business, new execs who want to keep their jobs focus hard on productivity in the first crucial months.

In a recent Conference Board CEO Challenge survey, chief executives from a variety of industries were interviewed about what they considered to be their top ten priorities. American CEOs identified their number-one priority as "sustained and top-line growth"—exactly what newly promoted officers of the company should be focused on. A close second: "consistent execution of strategy by top management."

Tasks that are more familiar will tempt those who have a tough time adjusting. Operations and finance people stepping into chief commercial officer positions, for instance, tend to focus on cost reductions and process improvements. Maybe they move from a line organization to a matrix or vice versa. Or they take out certain people and move in their own. Manufacturing people and engineers stick to their skill sets. They might look for new ways to sustain cost-cutting modalities. Finance folks, who are known for their ability to help the CEO cut expenses when projections fall short, look at the forecasts. Marketers press for the big idea and consumer engagement. Sales jocks concentrate on outside relationships and expanding market share. None of these strategies are designed to meet a trial by fire, and none will be sufficient to the critics eyeing your first 100 days on the job.

Begin and end each of those first 100 days weighing new ideas for how to ramp up your organization's productivity. In the nonprofit arena, that means developing new strategies for reaching out to donors or tapping new resources. In business, it means coming up with innovative ways to jump the revenue curve.

And do not let the distractions of your new environment deter you from A+ execution. There are plenty of smaller tasks competing for a new leader's attention: the seemingly endless meetings to resolve crisis situations (or, in many cases, re-solve them), meeting underserved management priorities, and the ever-present hurdle of human-resources issues. There may be upcoming regulatory inspections. Old and new vendors seek an audience. Analysts barrage you for new data.

The most successful leaders shelve the irrelevant meetings, the 100 daily emails, and the twenty-five voicemails. If you've exceeded expectations after the first 100 days, there will be plenty of time to catch up with nonpriorities.

NOTCH SOME EARLY WINS

In today's economy, if you haven't done something, you've done nothing. So even while you're formulating and executing your long-term plans to raise productivity, you should be striving for "early wins" on the job. Early wins build credibility and confidence. They confirm that you are indeed the right pick for the job, that you've earned support from your key stakeholders. Early wins energize your people, galvanizing them with the spirit to fight for a "yes." (And, at public companies, early wins get influential securities analysts on board.)

Early wins also tell your people they're part of a bright future. Lew Platt, former CEO at Hewlett-Packard and a dynamic thinker, says that success can be a matter of picking the right battles from the start. "If you can find a few things that were serious flaws in the organization and fix them quickly, you can establish your credibility as a leader very fast," he says. You can derive an early win from the turnaround of a failing product, from a creative new acquisition, from a team effort that raises spirits, or from higher profits and shared values.

In sales or consulting, major customers can be another resource for early wins. Because their money is on the line, they operate without delusion. They will want to learn quickly how your leadership will improve their outcomes, and you should want to meet with them to offer personal assurance and hope and instill trust. In the healthcare space, for example, this means sitting down to learn from patients and caregivers, payers, hospital pharmacists, physician specialists, and high prescribers of your product class. How, in their thinking, do they position your company or services? What's their take on improving your relationship? What will it take to enhance their loyalty to your mission or product line versus perceived competitors?

Of course, the value of your early diligence and goal setting will be greatly diminished if they go unnoticed, particularly by your stakeholders and staff. It's important to define and publicize the vision that will make your new administration a winner. Think of it as a branding challenge: make it a 100-day priority to brand your operation and to identify clearly where it's headed and what must be done to alter the course, if necessary. How are we identified in our marketplace, our community, or even our own company? Are we happy with that identity? Should we be adding or subtracting business segments or simply focusing on what we have? Do we have in place the right people, who embrace change and innovation, or the wrong ones, who long for the past?

Meg Whitman, the former chief executive of eBay, exhibited this kind of early action when she took over the online auctioneer in 1998. She quickly brought in a like-minded staff, expanded eBay's target sellers to include retailers, and instituted an insurance policy against fraud. She was rewarded with the faith of her staff and shareholders and a long and prosperous tenure.

UNDERSTAND AND EMPOWER YOUR KEY PLAYERS

One of the biggest challenges for today's new leaders is to get familiar with the people under their command. "It takes a while for even really smart CEOs to understand that it's people first, strategy second," says Michael Feiner, a management professor at Columbia University's Graduate School of Business. "That comes from experience and mistakes, and I don't think there's a shortcut."

It is imperative to track, benchmark, and over-communicate regarding the performance of key direct reports from the outset: you must get to know who they are, how they think, if they fully understand your vision, and whether they're ready to take on a heavier workload to make it real. Are they ready to face the new hand of challenges the economy has dealt the organization? The staffer who says, "I'm in over my head already, and I can't see taking on greater responsibilities" should be allowed to take those sentiments to another organization—promptly.

Great leaders surround themselves with people as smart as or smarter than they are. To paraphrase Jack Welch, "I like to be the dumbest person in the room when I meet with my most productive direct reports and consultants."

Figure out which of your people you can count on: which are top-flight As and promising Bs, and which are Cs heading toward the door because they just don't complement the new vision and direction. Keep the pressure on the As to maintain their lofty status and on the Bs to work hard to replace those above them who won't maintain the necessary pace.

W. James McNerney Jr., a former CEO of 3M and the current head of Boeing, was once asked what he observed about those who grew under his leadership and those who did not, and whether he could predict who they'd be.

"No, you can't always tell in advance," he said. "It generally gets down to a very personal level—openness to change, courage to change, hard work, and team work. What I do is figure out how to unlock that in people, because most people have that inside them. But they [often] get trapped in a bureaucratic environment where they've been beaten about the head and shoulders. That makes their job narrower and narrower, so they're no longer connected to the company's mission—they're a cog in some manager's machine."

Put—and keep—your most talented and passionate team in place, and you'll be on board for quick and lasting wins. Let them wander, and you'll endanger your early success.

Meet A+ Outcomes, Not Deadlines

As a new boss, you're going to come face-to-face with many folks who remind you that "this isn't how we used to do things." You can't dismiss them or their experience out of hand (even if you'd like to), but you shouldn't let their staid attitude hijack your agenda or working style.

Perhaps nowhere is this lesson more germane than in dealing with companies' blind allegiance to arbitrary deadlines. The time-honored tradition of handing in something, anything, on time is ineffective. The sooner you understand the negatives of that impulse, the sooner you can begin to instill that opposite attitude at your organization. (It's one thing you actually want to do in a hurry.)

Forget about managing time, and start directing the process leading to A+ outcomes. In this era of increasing global competition and decreasing amounts of available work, top-notch output is the price of entry. It may take longer, but consistently turning out a quality product that is superior to your competitors' invariably results in building growth today and a foundation for tomorrow.

Years ago, when I was on the client side, I once called my ad agency to demand that a revised tactical plan be in my hands by the end of that business day. I remembered for about a nanosecond that it was delivered on time. But the work was below my expectations, and I remembered that for a long time. If you have to choose, it's always better to be late with A+ solutions than on time with mediocre work.

While I'm not proposing that deadlines be ignored, I do believe our obsession with managing time—saving time and beating time—is a dated pursuit.

Time management is really about timekeeping. While timekeeping may have been useful in relatively finite settings, it no longer solves problems in the multivariate situations in which executives find themselves today.

To see why, we need only look at a few canons of antiquated workplace philosophy. A big one is making a master list—a list of everything you have to do, people you have to call, projects to complete, e-mails or letters to write, meetings for which to prepare and presentations to make. Divide and conquer and do the most important tasks first. The rest can wait.

To-do lists are important. I make them myself daily. But plowing through an exhaustive to-do list and smugly crossing off completed items helps no one and gets nothing done faster or better. Such lists often mire people in administrative trivia.

Another classic dictum of time management with which I find fault is to handle a piece of paper only once. (This includes voicemail and e-mail.) To comply with such an absurd conviction would require that we immediately read, listen to, and act on all of the correspondence and messages that assault us daily. This can lead easily to spending one's entire day, every day, simply responding. I recommend skimming incoming information and choosing only the most important issues for immediate attention.

Moreover, simply leave some decisions unmade. It's a bit New Age, but some things left untouched resolve themselves. Try it; you'll be surprised. Too many choices lead to exhaustion and frustration. If you want to stop racing the clock, get a new perspective. Start by first making only those decisions in a given day that are genuinely the most important to your business or family first, and have the guts to ignore the irrelevant. Stay with whatever you're doing, whatever project you're working on, whatever process you're trying to fix until it's executed to perfection, no matter what else is on the calendar.

In that people should not be concerned about time management, should they count on routinely working long hours? Probably. To get a top-notch result, it's likely that you'll have to work a little harder and a lot smarter. The payoff is that you will succeed: established and new customers will return and your chances of success will be greatly improved.

Hard to do? Very. It requires single-minded focus. Executives who run outstanding organizations have developed the ability to block irrelevancies from their minds until the job is done completely and done in an A+ fashion.

The underlying truth is that staying with a project, problem, or presentation until it's done right and done well actually saves time. This lesson is one I have heeded my entire professional life, and it is an approach I espouse today, both for myself and the people who work at my company. Our mantra: "If it's not great, don't do it. If it's not great, don't show it."

Time is usually not the driver of great work. Do not succumb to traditional, self-imposed deadlines if the work is mediocre. This is the most important strategic philosophy an organization can embrace.

And above all, serious issues in personal life and family always come first. If you are preoccupied with family issues, you won't be able to concentrate on the job.

Quantity versus quality? Quality is the hands-down winner.

Multitasking Has Had Its Fifteen Minutes of Fame

Another attitude you should purge quickly from your company is the idolization of that old 90s buzzword: multitasking.

Leaders need to find the path to truly excellent results, and the best-of-the-best claim that their secret is hardcore, end-to-end focus. To get to A+ results, sharp focus on the outcome at hand beats frenetic multitasking every time.

Daily life abounds with examples of proud multitaskers strutting their stuff: the soccer mom driving her kids to practice, cell phone to the ear, coffee cup in hand, one eye on Junior, who's about to strike Missy. And then there's the jogger weighed down with an iPod, a heart-rate monitor, a water belt, and, yes, a dog tugging on a leash. Silly picture, right? Not remotely like the "productive" world of business? Think again.

What is the operational situation at your workplace? Do you find yourself trying to read or write an important report in brief snippets between meetings, phone calls, drop-in chats, and business lunches? Are executive assistants advised to interrupt a meeting with key staffers if big-shot so-and-so calls? Do you shuffle through papers or flip through your BlackBerry while someone is trying to explain an acute challenge at a critical juncture? Do you rush through a meeting agenda in an effort just to "get it all done," neglecting the essential goal: getting it done right—one item at a time—in an A+ manner?

If you shudder when your teenager claims to be more productive doing her homework while listening to her iPod, texting friends, or playing video games, it may be because she reminds you of yourself at work.

Focus. That's the key word if you want to do A+ work. Sure, you can get a lot of things done if you're a skilled juggler, but how many of those things are really being done well? Are you settling for too much B, or even C, work? Are you taking shortcuts that can come back to bite you simply to be the master of multitasking?

Multitaskers may appear impressive, but research confirms my personal observations that their work falls short. In an article entitled "Executive Control of Cognitive Processes in Task Switching" that ran in the American Psychological Association's *Journal of Experimental Psychology*, coauthor David Meyer, Ph.D. had this to say about multitasking: "In effect, you've got writer's block briefly as you go from one task to another. You've got to (a) want to switch tasks. You've got to (b) make the switch, and then you've got to (c) get warmed back up on what you're doing." The researchers concluded that being unable to concentrate on a single task for, say, tens of minutes at a time, could cost a company as much as 40 percent of its productivity because of what they call the "time cost" of task switching. Business-research firm Basex estimates the American economy loses $650 billion dollars a year to interruptions and recovery time in the workplace.

Auto safety experts are now espousing that being on your cell phone while driving reduces your driving accuracy and reflexes to a dangerously low point. (Watch out for the coming illegalization of hands-free cell phones while driving.) And it doesn't get much better when you're taking calls and directing a meeting set-up or instructing staff. We were not created to do two things well at the same time.

The lesson is particularly important today. Dreadful economic conditions are putting pressure on employees to do more with less. The temptation to multitask is understandable, but as the leader of your organization, it is imperative that you set a good example (and maybe even send out a memo or two) to remind your staff that nonstop focus is still the coin of the realm.

Take a look at the superstars outside the world of business, and their secret of success begins to emerge. People who have met Bill Clinton at a gathering report that he looks them right in the eye, making them feel like the only—and most important—person in the room. Tiger Woods blocks out a crowd's whispers and camera clicks to sink a fifty-foot putt with big money and, more importantly in his case, big pride on the line. Did Wendy Wasserstein pen plays while listening to an iPod? Did Pavarotti hit high notes while slurping a Starbucks cappuccino? Effective, productive people have the ability to keenly focus on the task—or person—at hand, shutting the door on everything else.

That is not to say your priorities cannot change. Another mark of a good leader is acknowledging your dynamic world and reacting to the changes it throws your way. To that end, remake your most important to-do list each day, and keep your staff in the loop on priorities.

Near the top of any leader's to-do list are your personnel decisions. Granted, we all make mistakes, and that includes hiring people who aren't right for the job. Terminating an employee who happens to be a good person is one of the toughest tasks there is, but if you put it off when you know the person is in the wrong job and you've made a mistake, it hurts the company and it hurts your reputation. Fix it quickly. After stepping down from GE, legendary CEO Jack Welch said that in looking back, the biggest mistakes he made had to do with procrastinating about terminating people.

As a leader, your own focus affects the productivity of others. Think back on how you felt when you were trying to convey an important point to a superior or colleague who was busily checking her e-mail or taking phone calls. Recall how marginalized you feel when you're at a cocktail party and the person with whom you're talking is constantly surveying the room for someone more worthy of her time.

Notice how your energy level plummets when you're on the phone and the person at the other end puts you on hold for a long while.

One threat to your productivity may be your efforts to fit a round peg into a square hole. Make sure you enjoy the work that you're doing, or your mind is likely to wander toward distracting existential questions. If you like what you're doing, you're more likely to remain focused on it. If you don't, well, it's time to take stock and evaluate exit strategies, even if you haven't been on the job very long.

The message is clear: If you want to be a good leader, you must stay mindful, listening to the feedback coming from others and from within yourself. If you have a topic to discuss, then discuss it to its fullest conclusion. If you're running a meeting, run the meeting, allowing no latecomers or outsiders to burst in and add wasteful "time costs" with their interruptive behavior. If you're on the phone, stop all other calls and block out all other distractions. If you're writing a report, write it. If you're talking to an employee—or friend or child or spouse (extra credit here)—then really talk and really listen.

Developing such steely focus is a difficult practice to adopt, but you'll discover quickly that shallow efforts yield no high grades, no lasting excellence, and they will damage your performance. After years on the job, it will be your points of excellence—not the check-marked boxes on your BlackBerry or to-do list—upon which you will be judged a failure or a success.

CHAPTER 2
Craft a Winning Culture

CONGRATULATIONS. A hundred days have elapsed, and you're still wearing the big shoes. The numbers are good (or better). The stakeholders are happy (or quiet). The effigies are unburnt (or the smoke alarms are disabled and, hey, you're saving on electricity). Well done. Any leader who lasts more than a few months in today's volatile marketplace is doing something right. Take a deep breath and revel a little.

Now, wake up. Your staff needs you.

As head honcho, that call to action is something you should always be prepared to hear. Your job and your life are inextricably linked to the people you lead. The productivity of your organization or department is contingent upon your people's belief in the mission and their willingness to commit fully to exceeding expectations.

During difficult economic times like ours, leaders must show even more sympathy: you must be able to convince your people not only that your strategies are in the best interests of the firm but also that the best interests of the firm are in the best interests of your staffers.

Recall from Chapter 1 that motivating your team is critical from the moment you're hired. By doing your homework before your first day and notching early wins, you'll earn the initial trust of your employees, the board, and your major stakeholders. However, keeping them motivated and inspired after the novelty of your arrival wears off is make-or-break crucial to a successful tenure,

In this chapter, we'll look at governing philosophies and techniques that keep that fire lit, methods for creating the sort of environment in which people look at the clock to make it to their meetings on time, not to count the seconds until quitting time. We'll also look at the common mistakes that can extinguish that fire.

The key concepts to remember are to get a firm sense of your team's abilities, to treat them and their opinions with your highest respect, and to remain honest about your own flaws, mistakes, and intentions.

Don't deny your humanity or that of your direct reports. Understand and celebrate it. Come to work every day with a plan to get the best out of them.

Sharpen Up Your People Skills

Motivation is often considered to be some mysterious, intangible quality that blesses some individuals and escapes others, but your staff's motivation is, to a very large extent, in your hands. How your employees feel about their jobs and the amount of time and effort they dedicate to them is a function of the culture you create. Push them too hard, and you risk breeding anger, resentment, and exits. Give them too much leeway or too little guidance, and you might find your-self surrounded by a corps of B and C players.

So, it is essential to instill in your people two ideas: (1) an authentic sense that they have a critical stake in the success of the organization and (2) a valid belief that they have some control over its performance. If your employees fail to see the link between their own work and your firm's success, you have lost them and their momentum, and it will be tough for you to get it back.

This is not a new concept, nor is it one unique to management. In fact, it is the cornerstone of psychology professor Martin Seligman's learned-helplessness theory of depression. People who no longer feel that their actions matter will simply stop acting. They will no longer embrace challenges; they will hide from them inside a kind of defensive, disinterested shell. These are not the sort of employees you want your company culture to be producing.

Rather, the culture you create must keep your staff highly charged and engaged. To do that, you have get at what drives them, what is important to them at work. This is easier said than done. In *The 100-Mile Walk*, the book I wrote with my son Jonathon, we interviewed Bill Toppeta, the president of MetLife International, who uses analytic surveys to illustrate to his managers the wide gap between their "personal best" passions and those of their direct reports.

Investigative surveys like Toppeta's are a good diagnostic. They tell you how well tuned management is to the pulse of the people who truly keep the company running.

Know this: from where you stand, the most important thing you can do to keep your team motivated is to establish a culture of creativity, a cordial and collaborative environment that imbues value on the fresh ideas of its workforce.

Embrace Innovation and Execute

Tapping your staff's creativity is not just good for them. It's good for business.

Everybody knows that the best ideas rarely come from the top. We also know that people usually do not produce innovations while sitting at their computers answering e-mail, listening to voicemail, or sitting in on forecast meetings.

The creativity that spawns innovation transcends the daily grind of the workplace and often shows up in unexpected arenas. Great ideas come in dreams, from talking to people inside and outside of your business, from combing Web 2.0 content on Facebook and YouTube, from reading *Fortune*, the *Financial Times*, and the *Harvard Business Review* and an array of contemporary journals and magazines, from seeing new movies, traveling to foreign lands, and from scores of other daily human activities that are unattached to traditional office life in corporate America.

The question I put to many clients is: how can we reengineer your workplace to include innovation and actively stimulate the imaginations of your people? For many years, work life serviced production. Production is orderly and tangible, has concrete goals, benchmarks and quotas to meet. However, in today's volatile economic environment, with all its booms and busts, constructing a work environment solely around measurable output is not only dated but counterproductive as well. Such an environment produces the illusion of stability in the marketplace while keeping the minds of its employees dull.

Innovations flow more freely when there is no direct goal, such as with the development of the iPod and the Nintendo Wii. Innovations hurdle over goals and achieve something that cannot be imagined in the paradigm of the conventional business model. Have you noticed how a powerful innovation leaps over a staid strategy and becomes the new way of doing business? Today, more than ever before, we need idea assembly lines where innovation is manufactured—not orderly work sites where repetitive output is the desired product.

It is the leaders—top, middle, and bottom—that are charged with making this happen. Leaders must somehow find a way to unleash their people's imaginations and set them free to roam in uncharted territory. Leaders need to be prepared to put the process in motion and then get out of the way to allow the boundless creativity of their people to take over. Much different than the old time autocrats, today's leaders need to be creative facilitators—people who understand how to provide a fertile environment that allows for the sort of playful experimentation that leads to innovation.

At Flaum Partners, we have developed a brainstorming process to tap our client team's creativity called "Invitation to Innovate." These sessions are intended to help clients establish a rhythm of innovation and develop an ongoing practice that can put into place new ideas to ignite growth.

I suggest to our clients that they bring together a diverse group of people from their unit and meet offsite once a month—typically the first Monday, from 8 a.m. to 11 a.m.—with a different staffer to be elected the creative facilitator every time (not the boss!). No phones, no computers, no BlackBerrys, and no interruptions. A well-facilitated three hours is all a group usually needs to set off and dream about the next Big Idea. Anyone who says "let me play Devil's advocate" or "we've tried that before" is persona non grata. These are the preset rules.

During the "I2I" session, the group can focus its full attention on what's new out there—distill what they've been reading, seeing, and hearing about from customers, the sales people, the media, popular culture, analogous or relevant companies—and crystallize their thoughts from the preceding month. Next, the group sorts those ideas to screen out all but the best ones for the challenges at hand.

The participants then narrow their idea list down to the four or five concepts that best fit the organization's culture and have the power to promote what former Intel CEO Andy Grove calls a "10X change," a revolution that alters the business environment. And when they get down to one particular idea that makes sense and is executable, they are charged with making it happen. Finally, with plan in hand, they set the date to present it to the powers that be. The key for the leader is simply to get out of the way of the Big Idea and let it find its footing in the real world.

When appropriately encouraged and properly prepared by the company's leadership, these groups go into their sessions with the feeling that this is not just another job activity. They believe that they are actually driving toward the heart of a new business model based on innovation. That is an incredibly motivating force.

Your staff goes into these monthly sessions having really done their homework, fired up because they know they can potentially come out with a Big Idea of their own collaborative creation, poised to be executed in the real world of their business dealings. It is not just a workshop simulation for them. It's an activity that shows them just how much trust the leadership has in their creative abilities. And in today's knowledge-based creative economy, where workers are after the next big intellectual challenge, these kinds of leadership practices breed and inspire innovation. They also bolster employee retention and promote the recruiting of other A+ players.

For the leaders who nourish this kind of Big Idea thinking within the ranks, it would be foolish not to let some of their units' best ideas run their course—even ones that are not guaranteed winners. Allow people to fail, even during difficult times. Not every great idea can become a commercially valuable innovation, but some will be and they make the ultimate difference. Sometimes we get stuck in our thinking about leadership. We pigeonhole it. Leaders should be charged with allowing some chaos…just enough anyway to produce that "eureka" moment that transforms your organization from average to extraordinary.

GETTING YOUR PEOPLE'S IDEAS ACTUALIZED

If all goes well, the new leader and her team have come up with a breakthrough strategy that rockets the revenue number upward. However, the real challenge of the brainstorming process for most people who run organizations, consult, or teach management is the execution phase, the less glamorous and sometimes tedious side of bringing new ideas to fruition.

Many promising executives fail at the execution phase when it comes time to put that big breakthrough idea into action. Why? You guessed it: instead of pushing ahead to implement plans to "rock the revenue," staff, managers and the person in charge get folded back into the familiar comfort of less significant outcomes, voicemail and e-mail. Months later, leader and staff look around the table and ask, "What happened to that great idea?" That is, if they're around long enough to ask.

Research on creative brainstorming processes teaches us that the execution phase should be led by an outside process team, often with offices in the client's space. Another option is to assign the best and brightest to the execution team and relieve them of their other responsibilities until the project is satisfactorily completed and running.

THE NEED FOR A PLAN

Every year from 1988 to 2003, when I was the CEO of EuroRSCG Becker, a global advertising firm focused on the pharmaceutical industry, my direct reports and I escaped the home-office environment for a two-day "Dream Days" session, essentially a precursor to the "Invitation to Innovate" at Flaum Partners. We took that time to think about ways we could keep our competitive edge, reinvent the rules and stay ahead of the other companies in the healthcare space. We did this for many years, and it became the source of much of our innovative "breakthrough thinking."

In the beginning, the new strategies were carefully packaged by our meeting coordinator and delivered to me back at headquarters. We then distributed them to the various responsible division heads for execution. And you know what? Just as I suggested earlier, very little happened. All of us, including me, got wrapped up in our daily routines, putting out fires, and completing urgent but unimportant tasks—all activities less capable of generating income than developing a new idea. By the time we looked up, it was time to go to an important meeting or head out to the airport.

After the second year of these fantastic brainstorming sessions that went nowhere, we looked at the results of this not inexpensive exercise and realized we were doing a terrible job of executing them. The ideas were all there but the "doing" and results were not. So we changed the process and did a "Six Sigma" follow up. We rounded up some of the best-of-the-best talent at Becker and put these folks in charge of execution. And it worked! Our clients took to our revenue-producing strategies and gave us more business than even we anticipated. We eventually became the leading profit producer in our network.

The lesson for us and for many similar firms that went through these go-nowhere sessions was clear: don't spend your time and money coming up with smashing ideas unless you're prepared to move on them. The realities of today's economy mean you can no longer afford to waste resources. You must immediately get yourself an execution plan containing a specific time-and-events process with a tight schedule for benchmarks to keep you on pace.

The difference between the process we use today at Flaum Partners and the old Dream Days technique is that we now put a person or two in the client's office to work with their execution team to see that all the high-water benchmarks are hit on schedule. Experience has taught us that the space between the Big Idea sessions and the execution of the viable ideas is vast. Ideas have to be viable and fit the culture of the company, or the off-site session will fade into oblivion as a nice "working vacation."

JUMPING THE HURDLES TO EXQUISITE EXECUTION
Over the last fifteen years, we have identified two key hurdles on the path between idea and execution.

The most pressing and often-denied hurdle is a lack of personal and team accountability within the company culture. A great idea session is an exercise in futility if the company culture does not have an established accountability ethic. And what we have observed is that most companies have a hard time looking at their weaknesses and admitting that their culture may allow people to pass the time by passing the buck. To overcome that problem, we advise our clients that their annual performance evaluations should focus on their employees' ability to execute, as well as other attributes, such as working to get the best out of their people every day.

The other major hurdle to success, we found, is one that obstructs the transmission of ideas. Specifically, it is counterproductive to set up an innovation session without having all the key decision makers in the room. These are the key players who handle procurement, oversee brand budget requests, run the sales force, recruit talent, and navigate the regulatory and legal channels. If all of them aren't there, then the net result will be business as usual—you'll just have someone to blame for it.

Without representatives of all the different factions within an organization present, the turf wars that squash a great idea occur all too easily.

If, for example, the session includes only the marketing brand team but not key leaders in the sales force, then a great idea about how to better motivate the sales force is likely to be put down later by the national sales director, who can fall back on the standard line, "What does marketing really know about motivating sales people?" He can also claim that the economic slowdown has created a new sales environment that only "his people" fully understand.

In most cases, the roadblock comes about when someone feels that the expertise he or she holds has been dismissed by a less knowledgeable employee of the company. Moreover, the unique pressures of a recession can leave department heads feeling more vulnerable and territorial. Make sure each participant feels he or she has been heard.

THE NEED FOR SOME GROUNDING

After years of Invitation to Innovate sessions, one thing has made itself clear: they are not for every organization. Some organizations are at too early a point in the evolution of their culture, where they lack grounding in personal accountability and/or in the kind of direct, honest, and transparent interpersonal communication that is ultimately the most constructive for the business. If these issues are a problem, then we urge the client organization not to accept our "Invitation to Innovate," nor should it attempt to conduct similar sessions internally. The execution of ideas for these firms may have to be more authoritative and top-down by design.

This is another reason that it is so crucial to get an early sense of your interpersonal culture. Your people affect not only your strategies, but also your strategies to execute your strategies. Go for the winners!

Is There Buy-In for Your Mission?

With a framework in place that supports creative innovation, you've established the optimal conditions for a competitive and motivated staff. But you should be aware that the fire can cool quickly under a passive leader. There is a new bias against management, a prejudice brought on by the downturn's negative headlines showcasing the world's worst leaders at some of its largest companies.

Take John Thain, the last chairman and chief executive of Merrill Lynch before it was sold to Bank of America in 2008. Thain, who spent more $1 million to redecorate his office ($35,000 of which went to the bathroom), took home $83.1 million from his company in 2007, shortly before it became clear that his firm's bad assets would effectively end its independence. Toward the end of 2008, Thain lobbied for an additional $10 million for helping to arrange Merrill's sale. He eventually gave up on the money, presumably because he's such a generous guy.

Or how about Richard Fuld, the last chairman and CEO of Lehman Brothers? Fuld earned almost $500 million during his tenure. He took in $45 million from Lehman in 2007, the year before he was named as one of CNN's "Ten Most Wanted: Culprits of the Collapse."

Exorbitant compensation was an issue before the financial meltdown. In finance, golden parachutes were deploying even at the height of the real estate boom. In 2005, after former Morgan Stanley CEO Philip Purcell resigned under pressure because of poor performance, he walked off with $44 million over two years and a pension package guaranteeing him $1.2 million a year for life. His successor, John Mack, initially wanted $25 million a year in guaranteed salary, basing his figure on an average of what CEOs were being paid at four top investment banks.

It would be naïve to assume that Mack's focus on securing himself a small fortune before he started had no bearing on his motivation to do a good job. After some push back, Mack agreed to tie his compensation to his performance. It's usually a good idea to make someone show up to work when you've promised them $25 million a year.

The new focus on exorbitant compensation tainted the world of finance, and it's easy to imagine how the pervasiveness of the selfish culture became a sign post on the path to the industry's 2008–2009 demise.

When individual interests are removed from the equation, it is much easier to focus your team on results that benefit the collective. For example, Lance Armstrong is an inspirational athlete, but what puts him on top is the team behind him. They call themselves Team Armstrong and represent the innovative designers of his personal healthcare strategy and the bicycles, clothing, shoes, and helmets that allowed one human being to achieve a feat of unparalleled strength and endurance for seven straight years. Armstrong's team didn't just follow the money. They bought into a dream and gave their all for the sake of accomplishing something great.

There is no reason everyone at your organization should-n't want to dedicate themselves as much to the mission as the members of Team Armstrong did to Lance. If you've hired the right folks, treat them with dignity and listen to their ideas…well, that's a start. But as the steward of your company or department, you've also got to keep the workplace fresh and vibrant. This can mean reminding the members of your team why they got involved in the company in the first place. Part of your job is bringing back the love.

PAYING FORWARD PAYS OFF

Even if your staff is fairly selfless and free of greed, the practice of dealing with demanding clients or customers can often place artificial boundaries on your team's enthusiasm. This may happen more often in a weak economy, when every customer matters more. Veteran workers easily gravitate toward more established business practices, sticking with what works because it's safe. Take too many chances, and you might lose the customer's business or give your firm a bad rap.

But what if there were no downside to failing? What if your staff's big project had no strings attached? What if they could empty their playbooks and try anything to get their desired results?

Underachieving sports teams that pull off dramatic upsets often report being told by their coaches "to just go out there and have fun" and feeling as if they had nothing to lose. In many cases, these situations can be confidence builders. They can make teams aware of skills they once forgot. They also can get players to show up early to the next week's practice.

I advise clients that to imbue their team with a true competitive edge, they've got to give their players a chance to go deep every now and then. That can mean giving them a project that won't make or break the company but still has intrinsic value, or allowing them time to volunteer in the community, to engage them in something they can really get behind.

For example, when I ran EuroRSCG Becker, one of my top units was the consumer pharmaceutical product group run by Terry Gallo. The group had to jump through hoops to win assignments, and once they won a product, they worked 24/7 to make it perform beyond expectations. It was grueling work, and people often burned out quickly.

Terry and her group needed something motivating to work on. Luckily, we had a new, energizing challenge. They wouldn't have to pitch the account—it was given to them. There would be no financial performance concerns because the work was pro bono, and the client's desired outcome wasn't financial.

Our client: the New York City Police Department. In the 1990s, the NYPD had experienced a couple of unfortunate incidents in close succession: the beating of Abner Louima by police personnel and the death of Amadou Diallo. The department was losing the public's trust, and recruitment of new officers was way down.

Because of my commitment to and admiration for then-commissioner Howard Safir, I wanted to help the department with a new integrated marketing and public relations campaign. When Safir and several representatives from the NYPD met my group, we were won over by their genuineness and commitment.

With nothing to lose or gain, Terry's department produced one of the most creative campaigns I have ever seen. It earned the Becker team the NYPD Recognition Award and reportedly boosted recruitment by 18 percent. What's more, it gave our team new vigor. They witnessed firsthand the power of their efforts and the value of working for something other than a financial outcome. When it was over, we were able to transfer the energy generated from this pro bono assignment back into our commercial work and land some big new accounts.

There comes a point when people may have enough stuff in their lives, but they can never have enough purpose.

In Defense of Inequality

For all of your efforts to create a motivating environment and keep your people engaged, not everyone on your staff is going to contribute to your firm equally. This isn't your fault, and it isn't necessarily a problem.

Nature is full of inequities: Some fields get no rain. Some trees bear no fruit. Some parents have triplets. Some litters have runts. There is simply no accounting for many of the world's imbalances.

In your organization, some people will simply outperform others. This is a controversial but powerful notion. It will offer you great insight into the attitudes and abilities of all of your employees. It will help you identify your organization's next generation of leaders and your go-to team for high-level projects. It will shine a light on the people your predecessor should never have hired in the first place. And it will explain how there can be so many valuable people in between, saving your perfectionists a great deal of energy and frustration.

Back in 1906, economist Vilfredo Pareto noticed a striking fact in his native Italy: 20 percent of the people owned 80 percent of the wealth. As Pareto observed his world, he discovered that the "80/20 Principle," as it came to be known, applied in many areas of life. He was particularly fascinated to find that 20 percent of the peapods in his garden yielded 80 percent of the harvest.

Over time, the 80/20 Principle has been found to apply to criminals and the number of crimes committed; to accident-prone motorists and the number of accidents; even to the most-trodden parts of carpets as a proportion of total wear-and-tear. Less than 20 percent of the world's land yields more than 80 percent of all food; fewer than 20 percent of clouds produce 80 percent of rain; in business, 20 percent of clients typically account for 80 percent of profits.

In the 1930s, a pioneering quality-management specialist named Joseph Juran extended the 80/20 Principle to the workplace and identified what he called the "vital few and trivial many." Among the hordes of middle and senior managers on organizational charts, most are "trivial." The wise business leader knows how to find the "vital few," who have the greatest impact on performance.

Juran's observation has been corroborated by modern organizational dealings time and again. The bottom line? On average, 20 percent of people involved in a project produce 80 percent of the positive outcome.

During Jack Welch's more than twenty years of dynamic leadership, General Electric increased in value more than thirty times over to become the world's richest corporation—and the world's second largest in terms of market value.

Welch had his own version of the 80/20 Principle, designed to weed out the trivial many and focus on the vital few. He broke staffing down to a "vitality curve" of three segments. The top tier (20 percent) performed best and earned the biggest bonuses. The B list (60 percent) included managers with the potential to the rise to the top. Those destined to sink to the bottom (20 percent) were ultimately dismissed.

Welch was blunt and courageous, unconcerned with popularity. Results mattered most. Here's what he said about downsizing: "Strong managers who make tough decisions to cut jobs provide the only true job security in today's world. Weak managers are the problem. Weak managers destroy jobs."

Welch's focus on excellence and his ability to identify talent led to the record number of leaders who would leave

GE to run other companies. More Fortune 500 CEOs have come from GE than any other single company. (For the time being, we'll ignore the argument against creating managers who are so effective that they ultimately leave the company.)

Richard Koch, in his remarkable book, *Living the 80/20 Way,* describes the 80/20 Principle as "one of the most mind-blowing, far-reaching, and surprising discoveries of the past two hundred years."

"If you took a hundred people and divided them into a team of eighty and a team of twenty," he wrote, "you'd expect the team of eighty to achieve four times as much. However, if you put the twenty top people in one group and the eighty other people in another group, something much different happens. The twenty people not only achieve more than the eighty people, but they achieve four times more than the larger group."

How do you apply the 80/20 Principle to your organization? Koch recommends focusing on one or two points that matter most. "Find your 80/20 route.... Work out three 80/20 actions to get you started. Each one must take you a giant leap along your 80/20 route toward your 80/20 destination."

More specific paths to 80/20, of course, depend on the many variables within an organization. Who are your best thinkers? Your best financial brains? Your best salespeople? To whom should you turn at crunch time? Can you leapfrog the organizational chart and maintain stability?

Finally, do you want to be a Jack Welch-type leader in order to get Jack Welch-type results? Frankly, it can't be done without adopting at least some of the Koch 80/20 Principle.

That means not only making some tough personnel decisions, but also accepting a certain degree of inequality in your ranks.

You're One of Them

For all of the pressures of running your organization or department, it's good to be the top gun. Your salary is probably the highest. Your office is probably the cushiest. Your parking space—well, you get the idea.

However, there is danger in allowing these perks to hijack your identity as the all-around shepherd of the firm. Running a firm or division does not confer royalty, but it does leave you vulnerable to feeling too much like a head of state. This is a feeling that your employees can sense, and it is a tremendous detriment to their willingness to work hard for you.

The reality, of course, is that you must be the role model, working harder than anyone in your organization to keep it productive, competitive, and ahead of the curve.

There are a few small, seemingly innocent behaviors that you should avoid to maintain your credibility as a good leader: Don't joke about firing people. Steer clear of conversations about personal finances. Keep your temper in check—everyone is testing your authenticity and checking you out daily. And never forget your manners—always be hyper-vigilant about remembering a name, providing a smile, holding the door, avoiding a low blow.

The overarching theme here is: Remain cordial and humble. You're a boss. You're not a superhero. No one is. And if your team knows that you know it, they will respect you more. You'll engender more trust. In short, you'll look like the sort of person worthy of their best efforts.

CHAPTER 3

Getting Out in Front

L ET'S TAKE STOCK: The first several months of
your tenure were a success. By now, you should be
walking tall and into your first or second year as the
head of your organization or business unit. You've quieted
the early naysayers and won the support of your staff. You've
also identified your go-to people for priority projects. You've
shown you can wear the big shoes. The question now is: "How
far and for how long can you walk in them?"

What are you going to do to put your organization at the
forefront of its class or industry segment? Or, if it's already
there, how are you going to make sure it stays ahead of the
pack? During trying times, the gap between the top and the
bottom can be traversed in a heartbeat in either direction.
How will you keep the broader economic slowdown from
sinking you? How will you turn it into an opportunity to excel?

Being a good boss and a convincing spokesman will take
your organization only so far. At some point, you've got to
start innovating, sending out new products and services, developing new partners, and expanding your customer base.
The bottom line will always catch up to you, so it's best to stay
on top.

When Howell Raines was named the executive editor of
The New York Times in June 2001, he inherited a newspaper

with an unparalleled reputation. For all of the scandals, all of the alleged biases and cries of laziness, the *Times* was and continues to be the industry standard for responsible and probing journalism. For Raines, that was not enough.

"I made up my mind that if I got to a position of authority on the paper that I would change our competitive metabolism," Raines said in an interview with Charlie Rose. "Not simply energy for the sake of energy, Charlie, but because when you are *The New York Times* with the attitude of pride that comes with being on the *Times* and with the resources that come with being on the *Times*, and with the fact that very few news organizations can compete on your level, your biggest enemy is complacency. And I told the staff when I came down, I don't remember us ever getting outthought, I have seen us get outworked. We set out to change that."

The following year, the *Times* won a record seven Pulitzer Prizes for its coverage of the 2001 terrorist attacks, the conflict in the Middle East, and Wall Street. Raines would be forced out a year later in the aftermath of the Jayson Blair fabrication scandal, but his drive and push to keep the *Times* competitive left other news organizations in the dust, and the paper made history as it was recording it.

As Raines advised, you should always seek to raise the competitive metabolism of your company. If you're not winning, you should be. If you are winning, you should not only strive to defend your title, you should want to win the challenge by an even bigger score. Stretch out those shoes for the next leader in line.

Need convincing? Consider this. In their classic book, *Jumping the Curve*, Nicholas Imperato and Oren Harari interviewed CEOs of companies that did fifteen times better than the Dow Jones Industrial Average over a twenty-year period. Their conclusion: the biggest threat to a company's survival is complacency. It is the death sentence of any organization.

In this chapter, we'll discuss how to avoid that fate, how to get your organization out in front and keep it there. The basic ideas are to act quickly and take risks, to challenge old habits, and to keep tabs on the competition. Take note that some of these concepts may feel foreign or run counter to your nature.

So it will not always be easy, and it may feel uncomfortable at first, but with the right attitudes and practice habits in place, you'll soon find that competitors and admiring fans are asking themselves how you managed to succeed in one of the most volatile economies of the last 100 years and why they can't be more like you.

Forget "Ready." Just "Set" and "Go."

One of the consequences of the economic downturn is that the modern business environment no longer takes kindly to dallying. If you've noticed an opportunity, if a new idea has crossed your mind, then the odds are good that other leaders have come to the same conclusion.

Business simply moves more quickly now. Global indus-
trialization and new technologies have unified the world's
corporations, creating a diverse and dynamic international
market. This means that your business is now competing
against businesses in other countries in better economic
shape, with looser regulations, populated by cheaper labor
forces. If you think you can rest on customer loyalty and ag-
gressive trade policy, you may as well put up the "Going-Out-
of-Business Sale" banner now.

Even before the recession hit a fever pitch, businesses
large and small had become the victims of dated practices.
Remember Sharper Image? Linens'n'Things? Hollywood
Video? Circuit City? Polaroid? All filed for bankruptcy because they failed to anticipate new business environments
and the changing demands of their customers.

It's not getting any easier, as the 2008 downturn has
taught us. Business thinkers must begin to prepare their organizations for even more competitive challenges. The goal
is to be a leading company that gets ahead quickly and stays
there, no matter the economic climate.

The first step is to forget the idea that being perfect is
more important than being first.

Every leader of change has been bombarded by calls to
tap the breaks. "Whoa, Nelly," the cynics say. "Let's check
everything out carefully before we take a step." One check-
up leads to another, and another, ad infinitum, so the firm
can introduce a product with absolutely zero defects—a no-
ble goal, but a highly inefficient one.

Management guru Peter Drucker opposed this sort of steady-state managing. He once predicted failure within four years for any leading corporation that has lost its productivity edge.

And he was right. Half of all Fortune 500 companies between 1975 and 1980 no longer exist.

Before his death in 2005, Drucker updated his estimate. He said that it takes just eighteen months, or five and a half quarters, to go from leader to loser. In the global economy, even failure has become more efficient.

Why has the danger line changed so radically, and what does it mean for business leaders? What are they doing wrong that must by changed right away? What are they doing right that needs to be reinforced?

Tom Peters, one of our most respected and bona fide management sages, has an unforgettable way of summing it up: "The companies who believe in ready, ready, ready, aim, aim, aim, and forget to fire, are going to go by the wayside."

This explains for the most part why all those Fortune 500 companies are now gone. Their leaders thought their businesses were invulnerable, and they began to play what is known in football as the "prevent defense," a passive scheme played by the team with the lead, geared entirely toward not losing. Wisecracking football analysts say, "It's called 'the prevent' because you prevent yourself from winning."

Instead of playing soft coverage, companies and nonprofits should ask themselves how they can be more proactive, efficient, or responsive. Every business should always be thinking of ways to institute more affordable customization for their customers, whatever the industry or product.

"All of economics is information processing," Tom Peters wrote in his book *Liberation Management.* "Figuring out who likes what... and serving these specialized needs more quickly than your competitors, are what should steer your firm."

Peters and Drucker send the same basic message: competitive advantage lies in innovation, knowledge, and speed. Putting up unnecessary barriers to those ideals for the sake of comfort and quality assurance is counterproductive to your business.

Forward-looking leaders know and meet with their customers personally on a regular basis. This gives them a good sense of what is happening out on the battlefield. They are forever studying the marketplace and asking what they can do to ensure that they will own the number one spot next year. Waiting any longer would be dangerous.

STRATEGIES FOR THE COMPANY ON THE MOVE

Speeding the pace of your business will require certain adjustments on your part and that of your staff. The pace of business quickens with every new generation entering the workplace, and the need for speed is the price of entry to almost every industry, both to stem costs and to keep the competition guessing. You'll have to be more dynamic, listen more closely, and have a higher tolerance for change than ever before. On occasion, you'll also have to remind your unit's or company's more conservative personalities that you are wearing the big shoes and that what you say goes. For example, you'll have to keep your legal staff in its place. Lawyers should not be allowed to run your company. They're not innovators. They're not motivators. They're regrettably overtrained to mouth, "No, we can't."

Here are a few strategies and guidelines to get you through the process of accelerating your organization to winning speed.

Focus on the top line: Great leaders are almost obsessive about jumping the revenue curve through volume growth. They know that being persistent about finding new sales opportunities is essential to the bottom line's long-term improvement.

In a fast-paced business environment, it is all too easy to mistake quarterly results for success. Good leaders recognize the importance of controlling costs but resist the temptation of overemphasizing cost cutting. Trimming overhead can shore up a sagging bottom line temporarily, but the benefits are fleeting and can be ultimately self-defeating.

Superleaders wake up each morning thinking of ways to produce profitable revenue by strengthening their brand or service to gain momentum or by introducing the next product innovation to keep that critical competitive edge. This focus on "the next big thing" becomes infectious because your reports take their cues from the boss.

Maintain a dynamic management team: The best leaders recognize the necessity for top-quality direct reports, and in

Chapter 2, we touched on the benefits of identifying the most talented and hardest working members of your staff. Here, we'll take it a step further.

In the global marketplace, a successful management team is one that executes quickly. Your top brass must be hands-on enough, entrenched enough to be able to carry out your orders rapidly. That means they are attuned to their departments at all times and know precisely where there is slack and who is being stretched thin.

In addition, your team cannot be afraid to recognize that it has been barking up the wrong tree. That means not being wed to ideas that turn out to be flops. Dynamic managers are egoless; they do not hesitate to say, "This isn't working. Let's kill it and try something else."

Reallocate growth resources: Leaders who want to create wealth by growing efficiently are decisive when it comes to reallocating resources. They quickly identify their winners and back them with additional money and capital to strengthen their performance. They grow the market share of their best brands. If they have marginal operations, people, or brands they shut them down and reinvest the firm's energies where the growth potential is greater.

This may seem like an obvious point, but it can be easy to forget about that widget division in Cleveland that hasn't been profitable in years. To move quickly, you must know not only what you have at your disposal, but also what can be disposed of.

Breathe new life into the corporate culture: Every organization has a unique culture and tradition, and many of the world's best known are notorious for their distinct or rigid ways of doing things. In deference to these ingrained cultural approaches to the marketplace, many management consultants advise incoming leaders to take time to understand the culture and appreciate it. However, this is not advisable in every case. Many new bosses do not have the luxury of time to immerse themselves in a preexisting corporate culture. By dint of personality and management style, they need to communicate that fresh air has arrived and quickly begin altering policies and practices that have outlived their usefulness.

Some of these changes can be relatively minor, and these seemingly small shifts may go unnoticed by external observers, but they can have an enormous impact internally. To the rank and file, they provide some of the first tangible symbols of constructive change. In Chapter 1, we acknowledged the importance of early wins to gain the trust of your stakeholders, but getting staff to work faster, accelerating their competitive metabolism, can come down to conveying your energy and enthusiasm for change and growth. A weekly memo about the revolution can go a long way.

Take communications seriously: Superleaders recognize that stakeholder anxiety is greatest during times of change. Employees, particularly the best and the brightest, need reassurance that they will be heard and that their future is in good hands. Stakeholders, contributors, customers, and business partners also wait for encouragement. Although it has never been a part of the business school curriculum, being a leader today requires that you become the public face of the organization—and that means being the communicator-in-chief, too.

Superleaders take this role seriously, committing the time and effort to passionately communicate their new visions for the organization. They "teach" all the time without succumbing to the temptation of overpromising, preaching, or lapsing into wishful thinking. They also recognize the institutional benefit of communicating early victories, which build morale and beget additional victories. Act fast, but act confidently, too.

Keep Your Edge by Staying Edgy

Even as they effect change and institute revolutionary policies, many new leaders have a tendency to refrain from rocking the boat. This is a natural predisposition, particularly in the nonprofit world, but it is one you should dispose of quickly if you want your organization to remain competitive in the global marketplace.

Think back to the Greek myth of old King Sisyphus. In life, he was a trickster, but the gods got the last laugh in the afterlife by condemning him to push a huge boulder up a mountain only to see it roll down just before he reached the summit. And so it went, again and again, for all eternity.

It takes a certain amount of gumption to stick to an endless task, but persisting in the same old thing when it isn't working isn't gumption. It's inefficiency. And it's bad for your organization.

And yet that's exactly what most organizations still do. They get bogged down, over and over again, in valuing stoicism over inventiveness; this costs them dearly. As my friend Howard Safir said when he first took over as commissioner of the New York City Fire Department, "100 years of tradition unimpeded by progress."

Under current market conditions, the only way an organization can do more than stoically survive is to be innovative. Sisyphus might have developed a strong will, but he'd be broke in business. Work on becoming the anti-Sisyphus.

Sometimes we just lug things around because we think we have to. Take cans of paint, for example. Ever carry a few of those around? How about trying to pour from one without making a complete mess? Paint cans have been a kind of boulder that never went away until recently. And it took a new brand of thinking to get it done.

Dutch Boy is one of the oldest names in the paint industry, in business from the beginning, when there were just fifteen colors of paint to choose from (today there are close to 1,500). Dutch Boy was still pushing the boulder of the messy paint can while newbies like Martha Stewart and Target jumped in with designer paint, changing the essence of the market from utility to aesthetic. Dutch Boy's response? The company didn't have the brand essence to compete with

Martha Stewart and Target on the aesthetics of home design, so it thought bigger: not a new color, but a new can.

The company transformed the boulder of a can into a lightweight, resealable plastic jug that opens easily, pours easily, and creates no mess. Dutch Boy, through transformative thinking, got down to the real pain for its consumers, many of whom cared little about color choices and simply did not want to struggle with those darn cans. Not surprisingly, sales took off.

To compete, you have to look for that boulder you've been pushing and transform it. Examine the premise of the competitive set you are in, and ask yourself: What is weighing the whole thing down? Where's my consumer's or client's pain? Don't think about new features, gimmicks, or promotions. Think in terms of process.

What is the process that customers or supporters have gotten used to in the course of interacting with your product or service? What is the boulder, that pain in the neck that everyone in your company has come to stoically live with, and that you, by default, have asked your stakeholder audience or customers to live with as well? Whether your customer realizes it or not, she has grown very tired of living with the boulder. As soon as someone offers to take it off her hands, she will gladly accept the help.

Here are a few examples:

- Wal-Mart, Netflix, and Apple's iTunes digital music store now rent movies online, cutting out the need to drive to the video rental store. Not only did they speed up the delivery process, but they also saved their customers the cost of gasoline during a period of particularly high energy prices.

- In pharma, the birth control pill is regarded as one of the biggest innovations of the twentieth and twenty-first centuries. The daily dose was made easier by accommodating packaging dispensers, but the need to take the pill every day turned out to be the subconscious boulder. As soon as the birth control patch and, later, the once-a-month pill came out, the class changed.
- At the grocery store, the yogurt company Yoplait removed a less obvious boulder: the spoon. The firm's Go-Gurt snack, essentially yogurt in a tube, sold itself not on taste but on convenience.
- In fundraising, many potential contributors were often put off by being kept in the dark about where their money went. Now, many charities encourage supporters to adopt a form of micro-financing that encourages direct contact between the giver and recipient.

Organizations thrive by moving from one innovation to the next. Leaders know this and spend their time not by maintaining their lead, but by setting the pace.

As your industry continues to add bells and whistles to products or services, do not look to join in the fray and win the sprint. Instead, look to interrupt and upend the entire premise and win the marathon. Leadership is a long-term proposition, and being good at it requires more than the stamina to move boulders. It requires the ability of trans-formational thought to change the slope of the mountain.

Hear the Footsteps

Acting swiftly and being open to change are critical to re-maining competitive, but being Number One is only half about what you're doing. You can't forget about the other guy.

That's why great leaders don't sleep well. They wake up in the night with a start, imagining that competitors are stealing their best ideas, recruiting their best people, taking over their customers, and reconfiguring their best products. For them, there simply aren't enough sheep to count.

Having been mentored by a number of first-rate leaders, I've learned that the antidote to this kind of sleeplessness is to put your negative thoughts to work. If it sounds like I'm indulging my paranoia, it's because I am.

Paranoia is an indispensable tool for the leader who wants to stay sharp. The word might make you a bit uncom-fortable, but it's meant to. If you want to maintain a robust competitive edge, you have to take into account the possibil-ity that your organization is being spied on, stolen from, copied from, or plagiarized.

Greg Young, the former president and CEO of NeoPharm, a pharmaceutical manufacturer, tells this story: Before head-ing up NeoPharm, Greg worked at Baxter, a medical device company that made IV (intravenous) bags. There, he worked with a man who had a tremendous impact on his leadership style and his success. This colleague was convinced that someone was going to develop a delivery mechanism to provide hospitals with sterile water out of a tap at the patient's bedside.

At the time, Greg's company made one million IV bags per day at its plant in North Carolina. Greg's colleague was unshakable in his contention that while it was impossible today, at some point in his career, there would come a time when bedside sterile water would be as common as bedside oxygen, and their company's delivered-to-the-site IV bag would be rendered obsolete. The thought kept him up nights, and he made sure it kept up all of his colleagues. This leader used his paranoia to keep his company focused on not being caught off guard and on being ready for each new development.

It is easy to see the necessity for paranoia in the context of R&D and technological innovation. Where it is sometimes neglected is in the realm of the interpersonal, and that is a mistake, especially because game-changing business decisions so often come down to personal preference.

There may be no true accounting for taste, but keeping tabs on "personal preference"—the quirky and often intangible reasons behind customer allegiance—is a hallmark of my and others' successful business practices. At Becker, I challenged our people to construct an extremely rigorous performance-evaluation system, so our people were always striving to be the best in our clients' estimation. Besides the traditional internal evaluations, we also asked our clients to complete external assessments to help us improve. It was imperative for us to know whether or not our managers and creative people were connecting with their clients.

Human beings tend not to be confrontational about personal preference. They will rarely tell you to your face that they don't like working with you or someone on your team. They simply drift away, regardless of the quality of the work you've been doing.

That may sound like an insurmountable problem, but it's not. The best solution I've found is to add a little paranoia about personal preferences—or maybe a lot of paranoia—to your business regimen. This means paying attention to signals like body language and tone of voice—and looking vigilantly for unspoken clues of dissatisfaction. If your client or customer or volunteer force is unhappy and you can't identify any problem with the product you supply, keep looking—to yourself first, and then to your people—and make any necessary adjustments.

This is not easy. I have had to take people off client accounts not because of poor work performance, but because the client simply did not connect with them. And I have pulled myself off accounts for the same reason. It is just something leaders need to be able to do: assess and fix the chemistry, however difficult. And it is.

Be paranoid about new expertise, your people's contentment, emerging technologies, and products, systems and sales strategies that can knock yours for a loop. Be paranoid about how you and your people are connecting with clients and customers. Heck, your company's survival is at stake— be paranoid that you're not being paranoid enough.

As Kurt Cobain said, "Just because you're paranoid doesn't mean they aren't after you."

CHAPTER 4

The Leadership Instinct

B Y NOW, things are really popping and rocking at your organization. You've got a talented staff, and you're leaving the competition in the dust. From where you sit—and I hope you've gotten yourself an ergonomic chair—the future looks bountiful.

And yet looks can be deceiving.

Sometimes, no matter how competent the management, an organization will suffer an unexpected blow. The fields will grow barren. The toys will be toxic. The lenders will default. The regulatory environment will change. The economy will turn into a tsunami.

Coping with unexpected pitfalls is critical to being a great leader. Your organization will be tested, and your ability to come up with a solution, to forge a path out of the darkness, will be critical, regardless of whether or not the setback was your fault. Too many key managers have lost their jobs because they were made scapegoats during tough times. This is a fate you can avoid, but there is no single strategy for coping with unknown disasters. And you cannot spend your days planning for them.

What you can do is change the way you think about yourself, your business, and your industry. By developing a broader, more dynamic attitude about what it is you do, you'll find yourself in a better position to handle life's curveballs.

Of course, the right perspective will help you with more than just damage control. It will guide the way you approach your organization, your clients and your future. The right perspective is almost a business plan unto itself.

Now, no one can shift their paradigm overnight, but this chapter will offer some food for thought, as we look at the unique attitudes and cognitive orientations of successful leaders. These people embrace change. They show steady determination. They maintain focus on their clients' and customers' interests. And they look beyond difficult times, asking of their staff to answer economic challenges with ever more creative solutions.

This may sound to you more like psychology than business, but we're not really talking about business now. We're talking about you.

Three Cheers for Change

How you run your organization or unit starts with your world view, and that view is always in danger of growing stale. In fact, if you have not changed at least a portion of your strategy since the economic downturn, you are already way behind the curve. It is important that you continue to look for ways to enrich your perspective

Not that it will be easy. The single biggest human fear, experience has taught me, is the fear of change—it's more

frightening than death, Alzheimer's, or public speaking. We
tremble at the prospect of change on the horizon: starting a
new school as a small child, going off to college, joining the
military, beginning a new job, getting a new boss, coping
with the volatile environment of a corporate takeover, getting married, or cutting the marital cord.

As business and public sector leaders, many of us en-
joyed fairly predictable career paths that hinged, more or
less, on our willingness to apply ourselves within a fairly predictable set of parameters. Study hard, and you'll do well in
school. Work hard, and the boss or constituents will take notice. There is a reassuring comfort in these sure things, but
the world works a little differently when you're running the
show. Managers can study and work 24/7 and still find their
businesses flailing in the winds of change.

Of course, it is easy to embrace change if you're working
your way up or failing on a regular basis. But if all is going
well, where is your motivation to keep learning and changing as necessary?

Well, what killed the cat saves the leader. If you're not
curious enough to learn something new every day, you're
dead.

When I headed up EuroRSCG Becker, we didn't run daily
seminars or bring in consultants weekly, yet I'd often walk
around and ask people, "What new thing have you learned
today?" The responsibility to learn was theirs. We'd encourage it and supplement it through our internal Becker College
of Knowledge and our reverse mentorship program, but our

main goal was to cultivate a new attitude—a curiosity about new things that stretched beyond the immediate responsibilities of the job.

No book sums up the fear of change as succinctly as Spencer Johnson's runaway bestseller, *Who Moved My Cheese?*, a parable of mice and humans that takes place in a maze. But would change be nearly as frightening if we remembered what we learned as children from another runaway bestseller, *Curious George*? Curious George was never afraid to try something new. Did he get into lots of trouble along the way and make us laugh? Of course. But he also showed how much fun it is to set out on an adventure and expand our horizons. How can we transform our adult fear of change back into our childlike curiosity?

Take a look at some of today's advocates of change in the corporate world. Boeing CEO James McNerney cites openness to change as essential to success. Hewlett Packard CEO Mark Hurd, IBM CEO Samuel Palmisano, and Ebay's former CEO Meg Whitman have attained mastery at overseeing the execution of innovative strategies.

Such visionaries remain alert to the changing dynamics of their industries and their companies. They recognize that those not willing to adapt are quickly outdated. Jack Welch said, "Change before you have to."

However, it's not fear that motivates the world's top leaders—it's an inherent desire to keep things fresh. They are not frightened but excited at the idea of giving their inner artist a seat at the board meeting.

In the course of interviewing leaders across a variety of industries, I found that nearly all of the successful ones valued learning something new daily and were intensely curious. Howard Safir is a prime example. Over the course of his career, Safir went from serving as a New York City Police Department undercover agent putting away drug dealers to a desk job in Washington, D.C. There, he was soon called upon to head up the newly established Witness Protection Program. After mastering the new language of witness protection, he moved on to serve as associate director for operations of the U.S. Marshals Service. And then, in a surprising turn after a long career in police work, he accepted the job of commissioner of the New York City Fire Department (FDNY) under former NYC mayor Rudy Guiliani.

Safir's secret is that he never got caught up in his own success. What motivates him is the challenge and fun of learning something new and trying to be the best at it. After serving at the FDNY, he was appointed the commissioner of the NYPD, blending his lifetime knowledge of police work with his love for the city. When he retired from that post, you might have imagined Safir sailing off into the sunset (he is an avid sailor), or at least into another government position. But not Howard. He opted for a new challenge: entrepreneurship.

He partnered with former corporate security chief of IBM, Joseph Rossetti, to form the security consultancy Safir-Rossetti. Even there, the journey continues: from entrepreneur to major corporate CEO in short order, and from one

New York office to offices all over the world. What drives him is a simple but insatiable curiosity that pushes him to learn new things. He is one of the most accomplished men you'll ever meet because he's hungry for change. He just wants to keep growing.

No, I'm not pushing you to be the next Howard Safir. You needn't quit your job to lead a fulfilling life. I'm simply advocating an attitude of open-mindedness, openness to disruption that will benefit both you and your business. Keep learning, keep pushing to do things better, and you and your firm will stay ahead of the competitive curve.

I'm constantly urging my MBA candidates at Fordham to become change agents, to dare to dream. In one class, the challenge was to come up with an idea that would disrupt an industry by creating a totally new product or service. One team of students developed a brilliant but simple idea to disrupt the parking industry—a software system whereby people coming into New York City could reserve a space at a parking garage in advance at a set price. The project became a viable business.

Most people agree that the fear of change is a natural human tendency, but if you can overcome that fear, you stand the biggest chance of leaving the most lasting legacy. That said, you don't have to change everything in your life. Just because something is routine does not make it broken. That same daily cup of coffee from the same corner coffee man may be just what you need to give you the energy to change with a changing world.

Persistence is a Brutal Practice

Another critical component to a winning attitude is persistence, or an unyielding will in the face of setbacks. It is difficult to learn (and in tough times it is remarkably easy to unlearn), but try to name one successful leader who makes a habit of cowering when challenged. Go on, try.

Done yet? OK, this is one challenge you'll never be able to surmount, because those leaders don't exist.

Persistence is about digging deep to maintain perspective. It's the ability to quiet your anxieties and see a problem simply as territory through which you have to navigate. Leaders must be willing to work beyond any notion of personal limitations to do whatever it takes to get the job done. Great leaders do not offer excuses or lay blame on others for their problems. They do not add an extra burden to an already tough situation by indulging their frustrations. Leaders simply evaluate the best course of action and move forward.

When I invited Arthur Hiller, former senior vice president of Millennium Corporation, to speak on leadership at the Fordham Leadership Forum, he told the MBA students that attitude is more important than facts. As he so aptly put it, "The only thing we can do is play on the one string we have, and that's our attitude."

Arthur and I agree that attitude is more important than what has happened in the past, more valuable than education, more of an asset than money. We can't change the past; we can't change the fact that people will act in a certain way, and we certainly can't change the inevitable. What we can do is decide how we approach challenges. We can choose to see our troubles as beatable.

I wholeheartedly believe that the most important activity in any given situation is what's happening inside your head. Nobody but you controls whether you quit. Maybe you will lose today, but there is always tomorrow or next week or next month. If you are willing to tolerate the discomfort of rejection, the fear, loss, loneliness, or whatever it is that has pushed your buttons hard enough to make you stop trying, there is always another possibility. The first time your head tells you to quit and you don't will be the hardest. But if you can push through that and then persevere again (and again), you'll begin to create a new habit.

Here's a case in point. When I was recruited as CEO of Becker in 1988, the agency was on a downward trend, and they wanted me to turn things around. Neither the recruiter nor I had been told Becker was about to lose its two biggest sources of income and what was left of its credibility in the industry. Both Merck and Sandoz (now Novartis) were about to walk away. By the time I came on, they were gone and so was 60 percent of Becker's income. Down to forty people, with only one substantial piece of business left—Bristol-Myers—things looked grim. Everything I knew about business told me it was Chapter-11 o'clock.

So did my clients. When I began to call on them, they refused to see me. They told me Becker was over and that I'd be better off saving my reputation and going elsewhere.

The easy thing to do—the thing that may have seemed to make the most sense—would have been to quit. But I didn't cave to that impulse. Instead, we developed a "culture of persistence" starting with the forty people I had retained. I told them that with nowhere to go but up—believing it myself—one day we would have the top products in the pharmaceutical industry in our roster and that we would do it by being the smartest marketing and sales organization in the business. I told them they had an opportunity to prove themselves.

We formed the Becker BrainBusters. "Never visit a client without a Big Idea" became our mantra. When we called on a client, we had a new strategy for them. If they saw us, it was because we intrigued them with our knowledge of their business. And we became relentlessly creative about getting our ideas to them, despite their initial resistance. This work takes courage, so I told my people to leave their egos at home and to focus on ideas. In time, this became liberating—we were operating like an entrepreneurial start-up, and we loved it. We worked as if we had nothing to lose. We checked our fear of failure at the door and kept chipping away.

Our litmus test was a snub from the company that had stuck with us. Bristol-Myers did not invite us to repitch the business for Buspar, an antianxiety drug we helped them launch years before. After several phone calls and detailed letters chock-full of ideas (no e-mail back then), Don Hayden and Dave Whitehead, the product directors at the time, finally invited us to repitch, admittedly as an underdog, competing against the top three global agencies at that time.

Hayden and Whitehead saw merit in the strategy we proposed. We wound up winning the business because we came up with the industry's first compliance program.

At that time Buspar was competing with drugs like Ativan and Valium, antianxiety medications that worked immediately. Buspar took three weeks to work and its advantage was it was not addictive. However, patients didn't want to wait three weeks for the effect of the drug to kick in. That left sales flat.

Becker designed a public education campaign for patient compliance, making sense of the benefits of hanging in there for three weeks. Sales of the drug took off like a rocket, and Buspar became a blockbuster, setting a new trend for the entire category of psychotropic drugs.

Word got out about Becker being an idea agency that follows up with execution, and we were on our way. It was a great fifteen-year run from there. The capstone came in 2003 when Becker was named Agency of the Year and boasted seven of the top ten pharmaceutical companies in the world as clients. No other agency, healthcare or consumer, had as many billion-dollar brands under its belt as EuroRSCG Becker.

We were able to accomplish what we did because our culture of persisting, pushing through rejection and opposition, became our way of life. The secret was nothing more than hard work, smart work, and not allowing the nagging doubts in our brains and our hearts to stand in the way. We transcended our problems because we chose to believe in ourselves, even when there was little to believe in.

John D. Rockefeller, the first American billionaire, recognized the power of putting on blinders in the face of seemingly insurmountable odds. He said, "I do not think there is any other quality so essential to success of any kind as the quality of perseverance. It overcomes almost everything, even nature."

Looking for the Upturn

Your ability to ignore bad news will be put to the acid test during difficult economic times—not because you will be more immune than your peers, whose fortunes may or may not turn on the business environment, but because there is a kind of passive acceptance that this is simply the way things are operating right now, and there is no sense in trying to overturn it.

If you've guessed that this is not part of the winner's attitude, you're beginning to understand how top leaders think.

During tough economic times, it is easy for heads of corporations and nonprofit organizations to get caught up in the turmoil. We can wring our hands over the availability of funding or the direction of the stock market and calculate hourly the amount of wealth we've lost. We can focus on making ourselves look better in front of our boards, riding the classic "herd instinct" by cutting jobs and trimming expenses. We can fret over how the downturn threatens our organization in the months to come: fewer buyers, no bonuses, options underwater, layoffs, never-ending doom and gloom as the credit crisis worsens. We can do all of these things, and we can exhaust ourselves.

Or we can apply ourselves to running our businesses brilliantly.

At the time of the publication of this book, the 2008–2009 economic crisis appears bad and likely to get worse, but worrying and second-guessing will help neither you nor your organization.

Great leaders use their energy to the fullest during trying times. They hunt voraciously for ideas, track the flow of capital (tight as it may be), and seize new opportunities as they present themselves.

Recessions and depressions are excellent labs for this sort of innovation. At the turn of the twentieth century, John Moody began publishing his *Manual of Industrial and Miscellaneous Securities,* a compendium of market data for a wide array of industries. When the Panic of 1907 rocked the markets, his company went under, but he had taken away a valuable lesson about the importance of investor confidence and deep market analysis. In 1909 Moody began publishing again, but this time he rated the value of securities using a letter system derived from the early credit-reporting industry. Today, Moody's ratings are still an invaluable tool in assessing a company's credit and stability.

Years later, during the Great Depression, Charles G. Guth took control of Pepsi-Cola and used a timely and creative strategy to steal market share from Coca-Cola. Guth surmised that an economic downturn would make value more important to consumers, so he began selling twelve-ounce bottles of Pepsi for five cents a piece, the same price as Coca-Cola's six-ounce bottles. He also took advantage of the popularity of radio by advertising the price cut in a new jingle:

> *Pepsi-Cola hits the spot*
> *Twelve full ounces, that's a lot*
> *Twice as much for a nickel, too*
> *Pepsi-Cola is the drink for you.*

In two years, Pepsi's profits had more than doubled, and an early salvo had been fired foreshadowing the Cola Wars.

IBM also gained ground during the Depression. Under the leadership of founder Thomas Watson, Sr., the firm recognized that U.S. industries would be unlikely to dedicate capital spending to new technologies, so IBM took its business overseas to Europe, where sales soared. During the third quarter of 2008, as the downturn squeezed American businesses again, IBM's Europe/Middle East/Africa division posted 10 percent revenue growth.

Of course, the entire economy does not need to collapse to create tough conditions for an industry leader. Take, for example, Frank Yuengling, the former chief executive of a small Pennsylvania beer company named after his family. In 1919, Prohibition leveled the American beer industry, wiping out most of the nation's breweries. However, Yuengling survived under Frank's guidance by using the firm's vats to brew "near beer" and opening a dairy next door to sell ice cream.

Yuengling remained in business during a difficult period by using innovative thinking to create new revenue streams until the Eighteenth Amendment was repealed in 1933. Today, the company remains America's oldest brewery and a favorite brand among Philadelphians. Just ask Wharton students.

More recently, my class of Fordham MBA students came up with an ingenious new concept for a Web site to teach unemployed MBAs how to seek out opportunities during the slowdown. For example, since plumbers and electricians are now in greater demand (and pulling in about $80 an hour the last time I checked), the site suggests viewers start up job-training companies for those positions. There are several other creative ideas, including ways to start businesses to help recently unemployed consumers get their medications affordably. There are always opportunities for the entrepreneurially minded, the positive thinkers.

Even if you can't be upbeat all time, recognize that there is great value in being tested. Henry Ford, one of America's most influential entrepreneurs, saw merit in struggling every now and then. In his book *My Life and Work*, he wrote, "Business is never so healthy as when, like a chicken, it must do a certain amount of scratching around for what it gets."

Walking in Your Customer's Shoes: WIIFM

Another common thread woven into the success of top executives is that they use their clients' needs to motivate their decisions. Customers are the lifeblood of every business, after all, so your perspective must encompass their perspective. Put yourself in their place and try to understand how they define success. How you see the world must take into account how they see the world.

The greatest of deals are struck and the best of negotiations are made when you can fully detail to your client or target what's in it for their side. Your customer/opponent/recipient has to know WIIFM ("What's-In-It-For-Me?") to willingly sign on to a change. Leveraging WIIFM is how an initiative gets built. It is the central motivation for any new proposition.

Don Draper, the incisive ad man on the AMC drama *Mad Men*, is a wizard at WIIFM, anticipating not only his clients' needs but also their responses to his pitches. His rare ability to sell clients on an idea is portrayed as more valuable than the ideas themselves.

Granted, *Mad Men* is a television show based on business in the 1960s, but there's a timeless lesson here. Clients aim to hire the company that moves ahead and stays on the cutting edge and the one focused on helping them jump the revenue curve. If you're not driving upward, you're just a commodity firm, and there's nothing exciting about that. In order to drive the initiative, you have to show your clients that there is something to be gained—something for you and for them. As Don Draper says, "The day you sign a client is the day you start losing one."

The best way to win over your clients is to present strong strategies, expressed clearly and supported by compelling data, and to steadily communicate definitive results. "Excellence in execution is the only long-term competitive advantage," says Raul Cesan, former president and chief operating officer of Schering-Plough and now a successful entrepreneur. That is true because your client's satisfaction is the only metric that ultimately matters.

This can mean driving your staff hard to achieve client-centric goals. In a study of CEOs conducted by B-school professor Steve Kaplan and his colleagues at the University of Chicago, the researchers analyzed hundreds of extensive interviews with executives designed to get at what traits and behaviors were associated with winning. Their results suggest that the tougher the CEO, the better: Kaplan found that "harder" personal characteristics, focusing on performance, and execution are paramount to success. It may seem obvious, but often it is significantly more important to be loved by your customers than it is to be loved by your employees.

The University of Chicago report supports this idea, ranking "softer" teamwork skills, such as flexibility, enthusiasm, and listening, at the very bottom of the list of desirable CEO traits. Leadership is the closest thing we have in our society to applied philosophy. Real leaders recognize the need to be surrounded by ambitious, passionate, bright achievers who will champion a new direction. When leaders are in sync with their followers, both sides are transformed by the experience of having a focused mission—any would-be angst over the managerial hierarchy is supplanted by the desire to serve the client's interest.

The best chief executives in the University of Chicago study were a hard-nosed lot who hired Grade A players, set high standards, and showed attention to detail, efficiency, problem solving, and persistence. In short, they were precisely the sort of people that clients wanted to see steering the ship.

Leaders with persistence who can perform with excellence and who have the courage to hire great people are at the front of initiative momentum, motivating people to get ahead of the curve and realize better returns on faster timetables. It's up to you, the leader, to guide your staff in the best interests of your customers. Sometimes, that means looking beyond the numbers.

Gillette has been Number One in men's razors for so long that when the company made its last appearance on the New York Stock Exchange in 2005, more than one-third of its value was in brand recognition. Why, then, does the firm continue to cannibalize itself by developing newer razor models to replace its previous top seller? (It was a short trip from the Trac II to the Mach3 to the Mach3 Power to the five-bladed Fusion.) The answer is that Gillette is never fat and happy; it strives to anticipate the needs of its customers to associate with "novel technology" at all times. It's classic WIIFM.

"Courage is key to effective leadership, which in turn drives critical innovations," says A.G. Lafley, CEO of Procter & Gamble, which bought The Gillette Company in 2005.

It's one thing to understand that the customer is always right. It's another to realize that this should be the guiding principle of your business.

The Right Stuff

This may sound discouraging but, to some extent, a winning attitude cannot be taught. It's the unbridled expression of your willingness and passion to accomplish a goal. If you want it, you go for it at top speed.

Several years ago, I read something in the *Financial Times* that struck a chord with me: a feature entitled, "I want to be like you—advice for the would-be CEO."

In the article, Lucy Kellaway reviews the book *Wisdom for a Young CEO* by Doug Barry, then an adolescent from Philadelphia. The book is a compendium of the 100 letters he wrote to the world's top CEOs and their responses. Young Barry had always wanted to be a CEO, and he wanted advice about the ladder up, straight from the horse's mouth.

"The first incredible thing about these letters is that there are so many of them," Kellaway wrote. "The second remarkable thing is that almost all the letters are the same."

Almost all of the leaders list passion, respect, ethics, listening, teamwork, and lifelong learning as the driving motives for their work. Kellaway states in her review, "I don't accept this at all. I suspect the uncanny similarity of their letters is the fault of the leadership industry. This says that there is only one way to lead—the emotional-intelligence-coaching-motivational way."

Near the end of the article, Kellaway lists some of the things she believes to be true about CEOs, admitting that not one of these truths was found in Barry's hundred letters from the top. Here is a sample: "You need to have a huge amount of personal ambition to climb the ladder; you will work so hard and so intensely that you will have little time or energy for anything else; you will have an inordinate amount of attention placed on you; and the overwhelming likelihood is that your stay at the top will end in failure." This last one, she reminds us, is evidenced by the fact that many of the CEOs Barry wrote to have since been ousted from their positions for issues of performance or ethics.

As a former CEO, I can't argue with Kellaway. Running an organization is one of the toughest jobs around, and to do it well every day requires all the energy one possesses. To do this job well is a way of life, a practice, not a position. Being a leader isn't for everybody, despite the "leadership industry" to which Kellaway refers that is packaging the practice as if it were.

At the end of her piece Kellaway grows reflective. "If I were Doug's mum, I would have mixed feelings about his endeavor. As a parent, you hope your children will not want to be actors or rally drivers. Even more, you hope they won't want to be CEOs." Kellaway wants to make sure that business leadership is seen for what it is—one of the hardest jobs there is.

Barry didn't write me to seek advice about the road to CEO, but if he had, I couldn't have offered him a formula or a simple aphorism to sum it up. When I asked my friend Senator John Glenn what it means to lead, he said much of leadership is a mystery to him. He couldn't quantify it, yet he practiced it. He said he was probably able to do it day in and day out because of the level of enthusiasm he had for his work. As a military pilot, test pilot, astronaut, senator, and now, in his eighties, the active head of the John Glenn School of Public Affairs at The Ohio State University, Glenn's passion served his goals; his love for what he was doing and his sense of purpose and pride in it carried the day. His leadership was a natural extension of his commitment to the task at hand. The great leaders of history loved their tasks, not their titles. They put up with the burdens of their operational position because their belief in their missions was so unshakably strong.

My advice to Barry and to all young people is to find that thing you feel incomparably called to do. If the task gets deep enough into your guts, you might have no other option but to lead. Leadership in effect may become a choiceless choice because your level of commitment simply makes you the most qualified to inspire and teach others to build on your mission. But this is not an easy life that comes with a handbook for success (this book notwithstanding).

And if Barry cares about something this much, it will inevitably hurt. It will hurt when he can't succeed every day. It will hurt when he works long hours and gets home after his children have gone to bed. So quite simply, if he doesn't absolutely have to lead, I would tell Barry not to set out to do it.

If you have been running your organization, firm, division, or business unit for a while, you know it can be a thankless job, one whose pay is rarely tantamount to the daily sacrifice or the wear-and-tear brought on by twenty-four-hour stress. You live and die with your organization because you believe in it. If that belief starts to fade, you won't be able to maintain a winning attitude, and it will show. However, if you truly care about your organization and its mission, you'll be an invaluable asset because—whether or not you realize it—you'll always be pushing toward the next great idea to jump that magical revenue curve.

CHAPTER 5

Leaving the Big Footprints

S AY YOU'VE NAVIGATED through the rough patches, you've got the right people in place, and your organization is doing better than anyone expected. Say income is robust, and new ideas are in the pipeline. Say you've got the right attitude to lead your firm through the difficult economic challenges of today. What about tomorrow?

You may be on the competitive edge now, but are you positioned to stay ahead in the future? Are you training the next generation of leaders for when you pass the torch? These are questions that great leaders are constantly asking themselves, and satisfactory answers require some forward thinking.

On the day you were recruited, you were immediately playing catch-up, struggling to learn all you could about the area or organization now under your direction. You injected innovative practices, got your staff working as a team, fixed flawed policies, parted ways with C players and culled through projects that began long before your name was on the door. As things grew under your guidance, you may have focused on putting your own initiatives in play, changing work flow and staff to foster good ideas, or expanding or contracting particular businesses and brands to reflect the changing demands of your customers.

Now it's time to look ahead. Great leaders do more than repair companies and keep them rolling. They prepare their workplaces to be successful long after the day they leave. This goes way beyond long-term revenue models and the big-picture prospectus. Your best-laid plans can be scrapped without a second thought on the day you step down.

One of the most effective ways to guide your firm toward a promising future, one sculpted by your business philosophies and ideals, is by grooming the next generation of leaders. It's not easy!

For young people, business is no longer as attractive as it once was. Market volatility has generated a steady stream of morality plays that begin with high-pressure work environments and end in sloppiness or corruption. (Think about it: if you were twenty-two years old today, would you feel compelled to join the ranks of the vilified and the depraved?) And yet, business—your business—needs this young and promising group, the rising stars. The long-term health of your firm hinges on your going the extra mile to bring young, passionate, talented employees on board and train them for leadership positions down the road.

This is an attitude that should pervade your office. Truly influential leaders do not view their roles as confined to the people whose pay they control. Great leaders begin their careers pursuing a vision for their companies. Legendary leaders live out their days promulgating a vision for the wider world.

In this chapter, we explore three different avenues for leading beyond today. We'll look closely at the idea of a professional legacy. We'll discuss the importance of nurturing future leaders, and we'll spend some time looking at the pursuit of bigger goals outside your office. Our key point is to spend a little time each day thinking about tomorrow. It may sound a bit morbid, but if you want to be remembered for your accomplishments, you've got to start writing your own obituary.

Leaving Your Mark

As a young group product manager in the late 1970s at Lederle Laboratories (now Wyeth, soon to be Pfizer), I attended a talk by our then-president, Bob Luciano, on values, purpose, and mission. Though he would leave Lederle all too soon to fill the CEO slot at Schering-Plough, his message to us that day remains relevant, especially in light of the recent barrage of IPOs.

The question Bob posed to us was, "What is the legacy you want to leave? When you're ready to hang it up, how do you want to be remembered?" Of course, you'd like your family to remember you as being a loving spouse or significant other, a caring and sympathetic parent, and an empathetic friend and human being.

For leaders-in-the-making, the tougher part perhaps comes when you consider your professional legacy. What did I really accomplish during my career? What do the people who worked with me, for me, or over me think of my manner, style, and achievements? What did I give back to them? What did I demonstrate about values, or, put another way, what was the essence of my personal-value tutorial?

In my own case, I'm extraordinarily proud that my career was and is being spent in the pharmaceutical industry. It is the only field that discovers products and healing treatments from which every person on earth can benefit. Are there some policies we need to modify? Yes. Were there some people in it who didn't deserve the mantle of leadership? Absolutely. But, overall, this industry can boast an unparalleled legacy—its people are in the business of curing illness and saving lives.

As for legacy builders in other fields, consider Michael Eisner, a tough boss for sure. But look at his accomplishments at Disney: Broadway hits, movie creativity, improved television programming, theme park innovations, and so on. Consider also Howard Schultz of Starbucks, Meg Whitman at eBay, Andy Grove of Intel, Steve Jobs at Apple, Microsoft's Bill Gates, Mary Kay Ash of Mary Kay cosmetics, Wal-Mart's Sam Walton, and the legendary Jack Welch of GE. And, thankfully, so many others.

How about some great political figures that have left us legacies for which we'll always be grateful? Harry Truman, for the Marshall Plan; Lyndon Johnson and John F. Kennedy, for tearing down the walls of segregation; and, of course, the greatest of them all, Abraham Lincoln, for overruling his own Cabinet to go to battle against the Confederacy and ending slavery. These lists are full of some of the world's most accomplished people, but the good news is they are by no means complete. History will append them with now unfamiliar names.

Given that kind of opportunity, one has to wonder about the legacies of those whose lifetime goal is to make egregious amounts of money and be celebrated for it with their photographs or pointillized portraits in the newspapers.

Building a memorable legacy is, to my mind, the single most important thing we can do during our time on this earth. Legacy building starts with doing A+ work, nine to five, or longer. It takes focus, sacrifice, and perseverance—particularly in times of economic uncertainty. If you want to go down in history, you're going to stare down the challenges of current events.

It's really tough to do the right thing all the time. We all miss the mark occasionally. All too often, we don't give thought to how we want to be remembered. Having messed up in that regard many times myself, my advice to you is to get yourself down into that easy chair on the weekend or on vacation and contemplate that obit: What legacy do I want to leave? What does my ideal vision of tomorrow look like, and what can I do to bring the world a little closer to it?

None of us wants to be thought of as average or inconsequential. Not many of us strive to be "that CEO counting his cash," like those guys being hammered on the front pages of *The Wall Street Journal.* There's a lot more gratification in being the leader counting his contributions to bettering people's lives.

You can start by teaching your successors and spending quality time with your rising stars on a regular basis—at least once every month.

Hanging Out With Tomorrow's Leaders

Corporate life may have lost its charm factor with America's youth.

Just as Generation X was turned on by the outpouring of entrepreneurship that fueled the dot-com boom and the rise of hedge funds and private equity firms, Generations Y and Z have been turned off by the sight of well-heeled pariahs in court and the stench of rotting principles. Every story about the recession begins with corporate greed and ends in global economic strife. Can you blame young people for snubbing the business world when its most successful legitimate players saw their fortunes reversed overnight?

It was not always like this.

You may find it hard to remember now, but business was not always a field that sparked angry comments from the bleachers or ridicule on late-night talk shows. Until recently, an increasingly global marketplace had created abundant opportunities for managers at home and abroad, as the super saturation of other professional fields has made them less attractive. The rapid expansion of hedge funds in a weakly regulated environment gave that field an aura of royalty in a gilded age, however undeserved. And popular culture celebrated the traditions of business with renewed vigor in TV shows like *Project Runway*, as well as in movies, blogs and twenty-four-hour business news channels hosted by charismatic personalities.

The popularity of business hit fever pitch with Donald Trump's reality show, *The Apprentice*, in which mainly twenty-something contestants compete for a job with a six-figure salary and instant recognition. The show—along with its many iterations—is a testament to the fact that Americans of all ages were hell-bent on learning the ropes of leadership. And it's the young entrepreneurs, salespeople, and corporate middle managers once referred to as "slackers" who seemed to be the most enthusiastic.

The Apprentice portrayed, with surprising accuracy, the transition from apprentice to leader as a journey that requires drive, guts, speed, accountability, the ability to think and make decisions quickly, and to get the best out of coworkers, and the wisdom to know when to be quiet as well as when to speak up. Americans fell in love with this show because it depicted business to be what it essentially is—a study in human character.

The Apprentice showcased lots of individual stars and talents. However, to advance in Trump's organization, the participants had to show that they possessed what it takes to lead. What does it take? Well, it is difficult to distill a single trait from the eclectic winners of the show's first seven seasons, but the last contestants standing always appeared to express the best qualities of their competitors, plus an intangible quality, an X-factor that suggested they could lead. Bill Rancic, Kelly Perdew, Kendra Todd, Randal Pinkett, Sean Yazbeck, Stefanie Schaeffer, and Piers Morgan—these people were magnetic, competent, and strong. Their performances suggested they could be groomed to make the transition from solo entrepreneur (or B-level celebrity) to great corporate leader. (At the time of publication of this book, former Chicago Bulls forward Dennis Rodman had geared up for the title in season eight. He recounted that he had to jump through a whole new set of hoops to win in this one.)

From the show's well-hyped start in 2004, it was successful in igniting an interest in business because its cast of accessible, down-to-earth contestants sent a message to youth: this could be you. For all of the participants' quirks, they came off as real people, driven by a palpable desire to succeed. These were people you could see in business. These were people that maybe, just maybe, you wanted to be.

The Apprentice continues (without Dennis), but its popularity has been greatly diminished—not only by the inevitable turn of popular culture toward the new, but also by the tarnish the global financial crisis and its perpetrators have left on the business world. Unfortunately for the real world, the inference is it's going to be a little more difficult than it was in, say, 2004 to draw young, talented, and motivated people into your company. More difficult and more important than ever before.

Apprentice 3.0

Who are today's most promising management students? And where are they headed in business? Do we simply assume that great entrepreneurs make great leaders and that eventually these young people will learn to lead all on their own? I don't think this proves out. So how are today's bright, young, corporate and noncorporate game changers going to get the training to become leaders?

Let's go back a few years. In my early corporate life, top performers were identified early and then recruited for the internal corporate management training program. The basics of it were simple: We were sent for our MBAs at night and taught practical management and leadership skills during the day. Those of us who made the cut went on to become some of the top leaders in business and industry. Those were great programs, and many of them in some form still exist, but how can we get better at identifying tomorrow's best leaders?

One answer might be to foster a system in which unconventional, fertile, young, off-the-grid minds are given access to the kind of leadership training my generation got within our corporate borders. I think we need to create a widespread series of programs in which the country's top talent can be identified as apprentice leaders and brought through a process whereby they can develop and integrate the necessary skills to lead.

Two such programs in the areas of public service where apprentices are being trained to become leaders come to mind. One is the John Glenn School for Public Affairs, where students are taught what it takes to lead with integrity and serve in public life. The school features masters and doctoral programs, but encourages "on the ground" engagement with the broader community in its array of internships.

The other program is the Women's Campaign Forum, a nonpartisan organization dedicated to providing prochoice women with resources for winning political offices. The foundation also recruits and trains women to become public servants.

I envision propagating programs like these for the many twenty- and thirty-somethings working at startups and other independent-minded pursuits who have the potential to lead larger organizations. Emulating these types of programs in the for-profit sector will help ensure that our young and promising talent get the basics down before flying solo.

With the many challenges American business faces today—including unemployment, the need to retrain the middle class, outsourcing, and the loss of service and manufacturing jobs—it is reasonable to assert that unless we think transformationally and identify and train the best of our youth, we're heading for dark days. It is incumbent on our senior leaders to cast a wider net in the quest to make today's apprentices their successors.

WHAT YOU CAN DO TO LIGHT THE FIRE

Employee training isn't episodic like *The Apprentice*. It is an ongoing, daily process. Leaders can't only be great doers, they also have to be great teachers. Remember the old adage, "Those who can, do. Those who can't, teach"? Forget it. To be an effective leader, you have to do both.

There is always that cocky manager who says, "I can't be bothered with training staff, I have too much of my own work to do." I say: look out—that's a manager who will be quick to blame the new hire for not knowing the ropes at the big client meeting. It is also a manager who cares little about seeding the organization with winning philosophies and ideals.

Too many corporate managers believe that tending to their to-do lists and staying closeted in their offices is more important than teaching and training their greatest assets—their people. And, sad to say, a lot of entrepreneurs don't grasp this truth either. They expect their people to come fully seasoned and trained. It never works out that way. The most successful entrepreneurs understand that training sets a mission and clarifies the vision to the benefit of the company. In my experience, I have not met any young leader that does this as passionately and consistently as Myrtle Potter, the former COO of Genentech.

"The number one job we have as leaders is to ensure that we've got capable people working with us, people who are emotionally committed, people who want to get on board, people who can buy into a vision, and people who are willing and ready to give it their all," she said at the Fordham University Leadership Forum. "And once you are certain that you have that, your number one responsibility is to help these people grow, develop, allow them to exceed all of their personal goals, and take their careers to the next level."

A mentor is above all a role model. Leaders must serve as exemplars at all times. And no gaffe speaks louder to your followers than a moment caught off the record. Billy Shore, a former U.S. presidential political consultant who became CEO of the nonprofit Share Our Strength, says that the key moment in any political campaign is when the curtain is lifted and the true identity of the candidate is revealed as a result of some unplanned action. Shore believes that all the creative spin in the world cannot rescue candidates from their own missteps at that point. (Think about Illinois governor Rod Blagojevich, who was caught on a wiretap in an attempt to extort money for then-senator Barack Obama's seat in Congress.) On the flip side, the political columnist Joe Klein says that, if candidates work the moment properly, it can humanize them and give their campaign a boost. Think about Caroline Kennedy taking a bus to the Bronx—untelevised—to offer her gratitude at the Sloan Public Service Award ceremony honoring a secretary with forty-four years service at New York City's juvenile detention center.

These rules of the unscripted moment are true not only for political candidates and their constituents, but also for the leaders of any company or organization and its employees. The camera remains on even when you think you're off the record. And YouTube is poised to webcast you at all times.

At these moments, even more than the scripted ones, your people are learning what you are all about. It's part of your job to make sure you're teaching the right lessons. Your legacy depends on it.

Were Your Shoes Big Enough?

As we get older, many of us ask ourselves if we've contributed enough to the greater good. The developmental psychologist Erik Erikson said the minds of adults are grounds for a private war between generativity (a desire to improve the world for future generations) and stagnation (a tendency to ignore that wider world and focus on the self).

That conflict is more pronounced within leaders. Often exhausted by taxing schedules, yet having seen some of our best goals realized in the halls of our workplaces, we know we are capable of creating significant change. Charged up by this power, feeling invulnerable to a point, it is natural for each of us to wonder, "Could I be doing more?"

The answer almost always is yes. You can be—you should be—thinking about the future of the wider world and how you can apply your leadership skills to make it a better place.

While there are certainly those leaders who focus their days on generativity, the majority of corporate America is extremely adept at producing leaders who put their own futures first. You've read the horror stories. Angelo Mozilo, founder and former chairman and chief executive of Countrywide Financial, presided over a period of irrational exuberance in the real estate market and heralded a misguided expansion of subprime home loans. Mozilo's company was worth next to nothing when it was sold to Bank of America in 2008, and the devaluation was owed, in no small part, to his dumping more than $400 million worth of his own shares during the company's public listing. His punishment: a $56 million golden parachute.

Richard Fuld wielded a heavy hand in the securities fraud that took down Lehman Brothers, one of Wall Street's most venerable firms, yet so far he has walked away with a $24 million severance package.

The former CEO of Pfizer, Hank McKinnell, departed "unexpectedly" and received a tidy consolation prize: nearly $200 million. John Thain, the last chief executive of Merrill Lynch, took home $83.1 million in 2007, the year before the firm would collapse under the weight of bad investments and be acquired by Bank of America. Will we ever forget CEO Edward Liddy defending his use of borrowed millions to pay for executive bonuses at A.I.G.?

Such stories do more than garner lurid headlines. They turn stomachs. And perhaps no one wrenches the gut more than Bernard Madoff, the fund manager turned corrupt magician, whose elaborate Ponzi scheme made $50 billion disappear. Years of detailed fakery and exquisite salesmanship enriched Mr. Madoff and his family before the economic downturn caused a rush on his fund and forced him to reveal that it had all been a house of cards.

Cases like Mr. Madoff's do more than make us ill. They depress us and make us question where all the real leaders have gone. Where are the positive stories about successful people who really are making a difference in the world? Bill Gates and Warren Buffett, who've given hundreds of millions to good causes, represent obvious and heartening examples. Their legacies will last long after the ink has dried on the latest "World's Richest People" list. I teach and believe that successful people have a clear responsibility to "pay it forward," to invest in the well-being of people they don't know and who may be less fortunate. In stronger terms: if you're not paying it forward, you're not a leader in the true sense of that term.

Here are two outstanding examples of people who decided that it was more important to make a big difference than to cash the next big paycheck. Jeff Flug was only forty-three years old when he turned his life upside down. He had spent six years at J.P. Morgan, rising to the position of head of institutional sales, and twelve years before that at Goldman Sachs. He had three children. And plenty of money. But that was not doing it for him.

"I was looking for something more meaningful, more substantive," he said. "I wanted to change what I was thinking about in the morning." So in April 2006, he quit his job.

Flug had been inspired by *The End of Poverty*, a notable book by Dr. Jeffrey Sachs, professor of health policy and management and director of The Earth Institute at Columbia University. Sachs is well known for his work with international agencies addressing extreme global poverty. Sachs is also the president and cofounder of Millennium Promise, an organization with an extraordinary mission: "to ensure ours is the last generation to know poverty."

Fortunately for Flug, Millennium Promise was looking for a CEO just as he was looking for a position that would enrich his soul. It was a case of the right job for the right person at the right time.

Flug told me that early in his time at Millennium Promise he was leading a delegation of potential donors on a visit to Malawi. "We were greeted by a thousand villagers," says Flug. "During one harvest season, they had realized a fivefold increase in their crop harvest. They were building a granary to hold their excess maize. They had attained clean water. And they were beginning to build their own medical clinic out of bricks made out of mud. The village chief thanked me with tears in his eyes, saying 'Look at what we have done together!' I turned to my wife and said, 'Do you see why I can't go back to selling high-yield bond deals?'"

Here's another example of an authentic leader giving back. Patrick Awuah, a native of Ghana, was awarded a full scholarship to attend Swarthmore College. After he graduated in 1989, he went to work for Microsoft. Eight years later—financially fortified—he left Microsoft to enroll at the Haas School of Business at the University of California. At Haas, he assembled a team to study the creation of a new university in Ghana, modeled along the lines of a top American college.

Awuah's Ashesi University in Ghana, as of 2008, had 352 students enrolled from 14 countries, not including its study-abroad program. Awuah was among 250 people around the world who were nominated Global Leaders 2007. This award given by the World Economic Forum recognizes the unique contributions and potential of individuals drawn from a pool of 4,000 leaders worldwide.

Few of us will live up to the examples set by people like Jeff Flug and Patrick Awuah, but I daresay each of us would do well to let their stories—rather than the money-grubbing exploits of some top execs today—guide our lives. Don't you think our legacies—our real legacies—depend upon it?

Put the Right Foot Forward

Here is a great example of two philanthropists who flexed real leadership muscle to do the right thing. Sir Harry Evans, editor-at-large of *The Week*, and his wife Tina Brown, editor of *The Daily Beast* and former editor of *Vanity Fair* and *The New Yorker*, wanted to make a contribution to stuttering therapy. They persuaded the owners of the *RMS Queen Mary 2* to host a benefit for the American Institute of Stuttering. Some famous stutterers were invited, including Jack Welch of GE, John Stossel of *20/20*, singer Carly Simon, and Denver Nuggets' forward Kenyon Martin. For months, Evans and Brown worked tirelessly to make certain the event was a success. Together, they raised $1 million for the study and treatment of stuttering. They used their stature and connections developed in their leadership roles to give back.

Granted, not everyone has access to world famous cruise ships and professional basketball players, but the point is that most leaders have added pull somewhere. Use yours to help someone, to bring the world a little closer to the way it's supposed to be.

THEY WIN, YOU WIN

Doing the right thing is a lot like exercising. It may not feel good while you're doing it, but it always pays off in the end.

In *The 100-Mile Walk,* we tell the story of Nancy Lublin, a brilliant young law student, who in 1996 abandoned her career to follow an impulse to do the right thing. In a moment of clarity, Lublin invested a small inheritance from her great-grandfather's estate into founding an organization called Dress for Success, which outfits poor young women for business interviews. The organization grew, as did Lublin. Today, she is the chief executive of a national non-profit group called Do Something, which encourages high school students to do good deeds. She is leading. She is fulfilled. She is not a lawyer. What more is there?

The business world is full of stories of men and women who suddenly abandon the conventional highways of success to take more inspired side roads that allow them to do the right thing. Corporate engineers become the leaders of booming alternative energy firms. Fund managers create substantial returns by investing only in socially responsible companies. Doctors set up clinics in areas of the world in which medical professionals rarely set foot.

These people often drive older cars to smaller homes in less glitzy neighborhoods, but they are enriched by their integrity. They have done the right thing, and they are happier for it.

EVERYDAY GOOD DEEDS

My mom was a wonderful mentor and role model for me. She often spoke to me about doing the right thing; looking for the ways that each of us can tap the fount of integrity within us and channeling our efforts toward others. The lessons I learned from Rose Flaum were many, but the one that seems to stick in my mind throughout the years is, "Try to do something good every day." To honor her lessons to me, we created the Rose Flaum Scholarship Award, given to students who stutter and can't afford speech therapy.

And, please, don't forget about doing right at the office. Bill Steere, former CEO of Pfizer, often spoke about the performance review, the annual—and painful for most—office ritual in which managers assess their direct reports. Most managers typically spend one minute or so telling a subordinate about the good things they've done, and the next thirty on what they need to improve. Steere, however, focused on building up the positive attributes of his people, which is a lot more motivating (to them and to profits) than focusing on their weaknesses.

Extend this philosophy to the real world, and watch what happens—not just to those around you, but to you. When you're in New York City or Philly, for instance, and you see those street cleaners dressed in their Ready, Willing and Able navy jumpsuits picking up the trash, how about asking them how they're doing or thanking them for cleaning up your neighborhood? Make a connection, however brief. It wakes up the senses, both theirs and yours.

CHAPTER 6
Can You Ever Wear Sandals?

I

T'S GOOD BEING A LEADER: the pay, bonus, and options are great; the press is heady; the perks are generous. Some leaders get season tickets for the home team—maybe that luxury box at the U.S. Open every Labor Day—and, for the highest and mightiest, a seat on the corporate jet. Social interactions change, too—the welcoming smiles from subordinates, the respect of other leaders, the right seat at the board table, and the best executive assistant.

Even the job itself feels more rewarding. You focus on the Big Issues, the pithy stuff. Is the organization positioned well in its market space? Where is the company headed? And, as we discussed in Chapter 5, will you and your team be ready when it gets there? No one bugs you with spell checks, purchase requests, or event planning. The boss's time is too important.

After a number of years on the job, that same deference might trickle down to the members of your family. Then, you're rarely bothered with seemingly unimportant calls from friends or acquaintances, folks who just want to hear your voice or arrange to spend some time with you. If these relatively minor unscheduled stops in your day are not on your to-do list, they ain't gonna happen.

These people don't stop caring about you or wanting you in their lives; they just eventually stop trying to push their way into your Outlook calendar. If you want to keep them in your day-to-day life, it's going to require your personal effort.

THE FAMILY CONUNDRUM

The flip side of fame, glory, loads of perks, and extravagant vacations is that they often come at the expense of the very people with whom you want to share them. Many chief executives over time find themselves estranged from their spouses and children.

Mental health professionals say that divorce rates among hard-charging executives have reached an all-time high and that many marriages still intact require a lot of compromises—tacit deals that require the nonexecutive spouse to either turn the other cheek or cope with a certain level of unhappiness. In many cases, the power brokers feel as if they've just outgrown their spouse; but the lucky and determined ones find common ground and stay together—though it requires a great deal of hard work and, in many cases, marital counseling.

Family stress can present itself in any number of situations, but for chief executives there may be no more nerve-wracking crisis than the family vacation. Let's take a look at yours.

While you're still going on family trips to the Caribbean and Mexico rather than Disney World (albeit not as often), you're not having quite as much fun and you're not giving in quite as much to the luxury of "beach brains." How could you?

When you wake up in the morning, your first love is your BlackBerry, not your spouse. You're technically on vacation, but you're still being summoned for the "can't wait" conference calls with customers and analysts, whose concerns can be soothed only by assurances delivered in your voice. You might also be asked to mollify the fire fights that only your personal touch can hose down.

Remember your kids and playing catch with them on the beach? Recall that grand romantic dinner, just the two of you? How about any of the sites in—what was it again?—Antigua or Los Cabos?

No? Ah, well. You just couldn't put down that cell phone and dine in style, or drop that PDA in your sandal and jump into the water with the kids. Your spouse knows you care. Your kids will understand, you say.

They won't.

A piece of research I read years ago suggested that the majority of sons of successful fathers tend to go opposite ways. The custom used to be that we wanted to fill our father's shoes or surpass his progress. This study found that the offspring of successful dads are rarely as economically successful. They'll never have the job Dad has, the house he's got, the cars, the perks. Why? They are adamant that they don't want to work as hard as they saw their parent work to get there. Their opposition comes down to a simple mantra, "I want more time for myself and my family, so I'll take a different route."

I watched this trend manifest itself in my own family life and, to some extent, in the family lives of my colleagues. Of course, there always will be a few children who join the family business or Mom and Pop's company, but most will not.

When It's Bad To Be The King

When I meet my Fordham Leadership class for the first session of the semester, my first question to them is, "How many of you want to end up as leaders?" The usual response? "Duh. We all do, Professor. That's sort of why we're here." After the term is over, and the students have delved into the history of some well-known CEOs and heard about the hardships of getting to the top and staying there, we vote again. The result I consistently get shows a change of heart: only about half are still convinced enough to raise their hands.

As a reader, perhaps now a bit frustrated, you might find yourself asking whether or not there are any leaders who kept their competitive edge, who made it successfully through the challenges of their time and industry, and who managed to put their family first, all while putting in the time to get to the top and stay there. You would be right to wonder if such people exist, but let me assure you, they do.

Our research has shown these superleaders fit a particular profile. They are younger. They understand the agony of sleepless nights and 24/7 weeks. They realize their performance can slip when they are family deprived and relatively friendless. They're quick to sense when their spouses are reaching the boiling point or when their kids need to come first. (No one can fully focus on the next meeting knowing there's a sick child at school or a fuming spouse waiting for an overdue call.)

These skills do not come naturally to everyone, and they are often honed over years on the job. In Jack Welch's book *Winning*, he writes: "There's lip service about work-life balance, and then there's reality.... Your boss's top priority is competitiveness. Of course he wants you to be happy, but only inasmuch as it helps the company win. In fact, if he is doing his job right, he is making your job so exciting that your personal life becomes a less compelling draw."

"WH2"

Years ago, I set aside an evening to go to a Boys High reunion with my best friend from high school. We were looking forward to catching up. After the reunion dinner ended and we had said farewell to other acquaintances, he proposed that we go out to a local bar and have a drink. I blew off the invitation because I had a 7 a.m. shuttle to Boston the next day. Sorry, Partner.

We got together for a casual dinner a few months later. He lives in Westchester, and we met in New York City because of my "busy, busy, busy" schedule. We had a great dinner, and when we were finished, I looked at my watch and told him I had to go. Yet another early meeting with a client the next day. To my dismay, I haven't seen him since. He wouldn't take my calls.

About a year ago, I did catch him on the phone and was promptly informed that he felt my work and schedule were more important to me than spending time with an old friend, He was right, and regrettably, I haven't had the opportunity to tell him so and try to make good. My loss.

Even the most well-meaning chiefs are known to screw up, to make choices that hurt the people we love. The new "sorry" text message from leaders: "WH2" ("We're human, too.")

The loss of a good friend taught me quite a bit about the tenuous balancing act of success. My pace and paranoia about running the smartest consulting and advertising company in health care hasn't let up one iota. Instead, my defense strategy has evolved, and it now encompasses a broader band of executing managers—a cadre of A+ players and rising stars who get it and who, for most part, want attain that leader's mantle. Not everyone fits into the big shoes, but all of us benefit from trying.

GROWING SOFT?

A question that concerns me is whether our culture is pushing our best and brightest toward the "quality of life" side too quickly. Are we instilling too much emphasis on "life," rather than "work?"

There is no work–life balance in India, China, or Japan. Their rising stars strive to become as prosperous as their counterparts in the West, and so there's no letup over there. We're being overtaken by the innovations and business muscle of these and other competitive cultures every day. As of

2009, for the first time, Toyota is the number one automobile maker in the world. Will the economic downturn rally our innovators to help restore American ingenuity, or will it hurt us even more? If we ever stop passively watching Bloomberg and CNBC every day and start actively building breakthrough products and services that we can export around the world, wouldn't we accelerate out of our economic downturn mess a lot sooner?

Kind of puts the whole work–life balance quandary into a questionable perspective, though I doubt my buddy from Boys High would agree.

Learning to Pick Your Battles

A few years ago, I had a personal wake-up call, one that I related in *The 100-Mile Walk*, that altered my perspective on the wisdom of taking on every challenge that came my way. It's one of those life's lessons that bears repeating.

I have always been a fierce competitor. When I was younger, business was like an obstacle course to me. I couldn't wait to climb over the next wall, hop through the tires, jump over the water. All I saw was the finish line. If I couldn't scale the wall, I'd plow through it. It was all about getting there, no matter what stood in my way. It's how I moved from corporate product manager to CEO of one of the world's largest global healthcare advertising networks. To my mind, the legendary football coach Vince Lombardi had gotten it right when he said, "Winning isn't everything, it's the only thing."

Years later, after trading up a few shoe sizes, I found my-self walking into one of the most beautiful office lobbies in Manhattan for a board of directors interview. Before I reached the elevators, an impeccably tailored security guard politely noted my laptop and indicated his need to inspect it. He handled it with a gentleness I have yet to see in a New York airport.

In the marble-floored elevator, I watched the numbers quickly shoot up to twenty-three. Stepping off the elevator, I was greeted by my host and led into an oak-paneled board-room. A lunch catered by the Four Seasons was on the table, and my host poured me an iced tea. This was old school—no women, no people of color, no one under fifty, just an old-time board of directors with a sense of its own importance and a taste for the finer things.

The view from the windows was spectacular, the best in the city. The room, the setting, the finery—they all said one thing: this was clearly the most prestigious board I had ever been invited to join. It was the clubby sort you imagine exists but aren't quite sure is real. A white cloth napkin was spread across my lap and a drink placed in my hand, as my host be-gan making small talk. The CEO of this NYSE-listed com-pany was a colleague from years past who wanted me on the board, as did several other directors. This was no interview; it was a lunch among colleagues of equal stature and power—or so I thought.

Just as I was beginning to relax, the search committee head began grilling me about the weight and nature of my potential contributions. He was a personality I recognized from one of television's talking-head news shows. He loved to hear himself speak between commercials, and it seemed he had a script in front of him then. His celebrity status sufficiently intimidated the other directors, who sat by as he worked up to a rant.

I had a couple of choices. My usual response would have been to engage in combat with such an individual, to put him in his place with my knowledge of the drug industry, confident of my record and performance. I would treat him as a water hazard or a wall and go around him or over him.

Contemplating what I would say when he finally shut his mouth, a new thought occurred to me, one I had never considered before: I could just leave.

After you've been in management for thirty-five years, your intuition tells you which people are open to new ideas and which just like to hear themselves talk, which like to grow their egos instead of their companies. You also become attuned to a company's culture—particularly, whether innovation is welcome or not. I took a look around, felt the weight of the crystal Waterford glass in my hand, then set it down on the slate coaster on the antique mahogany table. I felt myself rise from my chair. I couldn't believe what I was doing. Where was the old fighter? The Lombardi acolyte trained to win at all costs?

I stood, buttoned my jacket, and smiled as I addressed

the group: "Being on a board is a lot of work. I believe in this company and what the CEO is doing, and I want it to thrive. That's why I'm here. Having said that, please understand my time is valuable to me, and I've been around too long to spend it with certain people I don't enjoy. I'm not enjoying this now, and I doubt I would in the future."

And then I did something I had never done before. I turned and walked out. My good friend, the CEO, intercepted me at the elevator and pleaded with me to reconsider. I patted him on the back and left.

Through the lobby, I sailed out onto a midtown street, buzzing with life. I spotted a cigar shop and soon emerged to light up before the MetLife Building amidst the energy surrounding me.

After all those years on the obstacle course, I may finally have learned the hardest lesson of all. Leaders play to win, of course, but there are times when it doesn't pay to play. To extend the Lombardi metaphor, winning the Super Bowl is arguably more important than winning a Week Seventeen matchup against the underdog, particularly when you've locked up the division, home-field advantage and a first-round bye.

While I was puffing on my cigar still trying to process what I had just done, a teenaged skateboard jock in urban street clothes approached me. "Got the time, chief?" he asked.

Smiling at his question and back at him, I looked at my watch. "Only for important things," I said.

Untying Your Laces

Vacation, I finally learned, is a meaningful thing.

As the former CEO and then Chairman of French-owned EuroRSCG Becker, I spent a lot of time in Paris, one of the world's most beloved spots in which to take time off.

I was making regular trips to meet with my company's officials. It was a wild travel schedule, but I eventually settled into a rhythm. With my laptop and PowerPoint presentations in tow, I was whisked from my office in lower Manhattan to JFK Airport onto an AirFrance flight (a EuroRSCG client) to Paris, replete with my fair share of Ambien sleep capsules (product of a prospective client) in my shirt pocket.

A driver, in his smart black suit, was always there at Charles de Gaulle airport to meet me. Off we drove to Cedex, outside of Paris, where Havas, my parent company's headquarters, was located. Once there, my folks joined the team in the conference room, set up our equipment, had a great croissant and coffee, and gave our two-hour recap of the previous quarter and our outlook for the next one. Meetings continued throughout the day with the CEO, CFO, and other agency heads, followed by dinner and our overnight stay at an awful Marriott nearby.

The next day, the driver appeared at 6 a.m. to drive me back to Charles de Gaulle for my flight back to New York (thank goodness for Ambien). My view of Paris over those many years was through the backseat window of the limo—if I happened to peek up from my computer or BlackBerry to check out the Eiffel Tower or the Arc de Triomphe.

Over the summer of 2007, my wife Mechele and I took our eldest grandchild, Rebecca, to Paris for her thirteenth birthday. Rebecca is a bright and beautiful fashionista, so where else but Paris? Mechele, being a Francophile, was thrilled as well, but I was not. I was hoping for Tuscany or the Algarve, but Rebecca was calling the shots on this one. Paris again? Ugh! My passport had more "France" stamps in it than a wine store. It was like a trader taking an exotic vacation to lower Manhattan.

But what a rejuvenating experience it turned out to be. With my wife and granddaughter, I was actually on vacation, and seeing Paris for what felt like the first time. There was no computer in my pack, no business to conduct—only unscheduled fun and seeing Paris through Rebecca's young eyes. The Musée D'Orsay, climbing the Arc de Triomphe, shopping in Bon Marché, dining at the Café Marley in the Louvre and at Au Bon Accueil. Vive la France!

Flying back, I thought about this special vacation and all I had missed out on these many years. Like so many of my colleagues, I have a hard time escaping the demands that come with running a company, each day thinking about how to maintain that competitive edge. With all the issues that come up—helping employees with various tasks, staying on top of the most cutting-edge acquisitions, being there to handle important customers' issues—how does one ever go on a stress-free holiday? How do you travel today Black-Berry-free?

Like so many senior executives I know, I tended to act the part of the carefree vacationer, but I always managed to sneak away to make that phone call or get back on my PDA. Could I have become a better golfer without my cell phone on? Maybe (but only maybe). A more tuned-in traveler, a more attentive listener? For sure.

ONE MORE REASON TO TAKE A BREAK

"Perspective" is a term that rarely surfaces in leadership articles. We spend more of our time analyzing life's challenges than trying to contextualize them. What I've learned is that leaders must train their focus on "brainrest." Perspective is gained when the venue changes dramatically and you have enough distance to remove yourself mentally from the usual work tensions and concerns. A great vacation can be a perspective refresher, allowing you to reset your priorities around family and friends and maybe even ponder the next chapter of your life. These are ideas that are sometimes tough to embrace when you're knee deep in the weeds of work. Yet these are the things that make us more human and help us to create the legacies we want to impart to our loved ones.

Make sure to take a moment each day and see the world through the eyes of your family, friends, and employees because at some point, you're going to want to take off the big shoes. And you're going to need help finding your sandals.

Afterword

LEADING A CORPORATION, business unit, or non-profit organization is like walking a straight line in an earthquake. Just when you think you've found your balance, a tremor can put you on your rear end. That is why the most enduring lessons of leadership have more to do with effective work habits and interpersonal relationships than spreadsheets and flow charts. Numbers change, but the tenets of being a good leader do not.

In this book, we've taken a journey through the career of a leader to identify a few underlying themes of wearing the big shoes. We began with the idea that good leadership starts with personal preparation and the ability to filter out the important issues from the mundane. In the second chapter, we looked at techniques to win over your staff and keep them motivated and at full speed toward the mission. In the third chapter, we talked about the importance of risk taking and keeping an eye on the competition to get ahead and stay ahead of the pack. In the fourth, we talked about establishing the right mindset for your office: being flexible but also steadfast about the mission and the needs of your customers. We then turned our attention to the future and discussed grooming the next set of leaders, and we concluded with a perspective on work–life balance.

While we primarily chose modern examples to illustrate these points, the ideas and the philosophies behind them are timeless. Personal responsibility and preparedness, empathy and honesty, devotion and perseverance, vision and perspective. These are the transcendent hallmarks of great leaders. These are the traits that will set you apart, create a lasting legacy, and carry you through even the most troubled times.

As we've seen, the world can change in an instant. Your organization will always look to its highest post for guidance. Wearing the big shoes means being a leader for all seasons. It means being humble, being innovative, and being ready to wake up to a whole new landscape. If you can embrace those ideals, and work harder and smarter than your competitors, you will lead today and well into tomorrow.

Acknowledgments

B ig Shoes: How Successful Leaders Grow Into New Roles emanated from my listening to and observing the rising stars both at Flaum Partners and in the Fordham Leadership Forum at the Fordham Graduate School of Business.

Much of their input and shared reflection I use as fodder for the monthly columns that I write for the American Management Association and *Pharmaceutical Executive.* Readers of these columns over the years have encouraged me to expand my thinking into a short playbook on how to grow into a new job and be successful enough to be promoted. Two especially provocative questions I've been asked formed the basis for this book: "Now that I've been promoted, how do I show my superiors they made the right decision?" and "What can I do to demonstrate my prowess in the new job and win the next opportunity?"

In formulating the concepts for *Big Shoes*, I knew I needed around me the people who as a rule expand my thinking on the motivations and inner turmoil of rising stars with leadership ambitions: I began with my thirty- and forty-something clients at Flaum Partners. Listening to their issues on work–life balance and their concerns about innovation in their respective companies provided great insights. I also asked my friend at AMA, Bob Smith, to read an early draft of *Big Shoes* and his critique was extraordinarily helpful.

Jeff Belle at Amazon was a fount of useful information. Jeff aided us in our thinking about thrust and audience. I can't say enough about his warmth and knowledge. Lisa Pollione, my executive assistant was, as always, constantly there to part the troubled waters. The words "No, I can't" or "I just don't have the time" simply aren't in her vocabulary. I'm fortunate as well to thank Mark Glassman, Gina Phelan, and Dan Tesser, whose suggestions and assistance were invaluable in helping me set the tone of this book.

Finally, and most importantly, I want to acknowledge my wife and editor, Mechele Flaum, who labored over the manuscript word by word and brought its meaning to fruition. She's an inspiration.

I'm just a lucky guy!

3931485

Made in the USA